Basic Stuff That Everyone Should Know

LLOYD LIM

ISBN: 146809341X
ISBN 13: 9781468093414

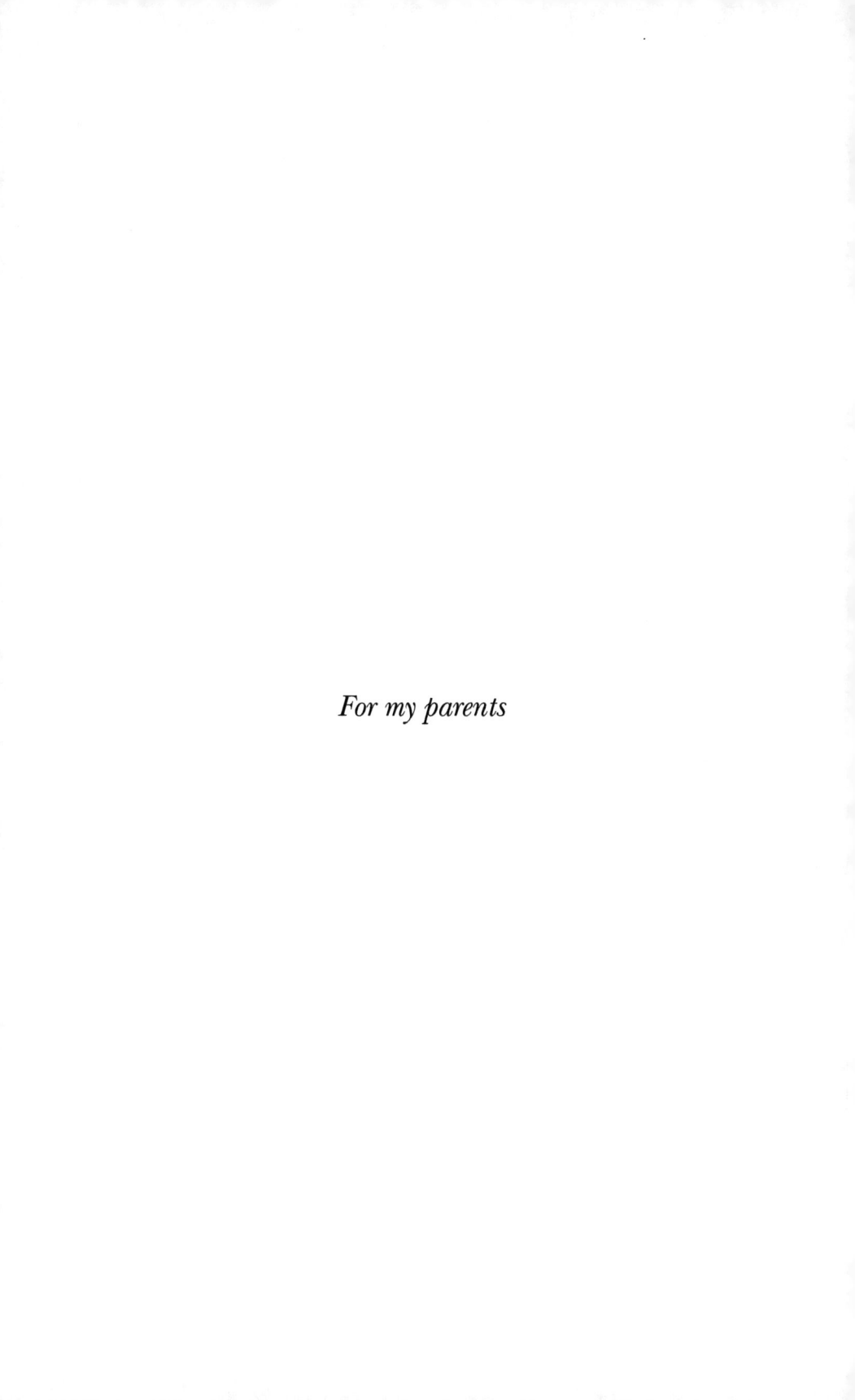

For my parents

Acknowledgment

*My colleague Samuel Thomsen commented
on a draft of this book.*

Table of Contents

Introduction

This is a book that teaches basic stuff that everyone should know about our system. It will be particularly useful to someone who has not gone to college, but can even be useful to a college graduate, depending on what courses he took. I have worked in the government for seventeen years and have dealt with the public every day, and I have found that many people do not have a grasp of all aspects of our system, mainly because our educational system is inconsistent about teaching practical things. If you know the basics, then the rest is just a matter of picking up trivia. But if you don't know the basics, then navigating the system can be problematic. This book attempts to a lay a strong foundation for building a good understanding of the system we live in.

Our education system trains people to be specialists, and our careers continue that specialization. What is needed is a way for people to become generalists so that they can handle anything that is thrown at them. This book is designed to help you become a generalist by learning basic stuff from a variety of different areas. This book is a collection of very short essays, each of which is a primer in a given subject area. Because the essays are short and I have tried to get to the point quickly, they are easy to read.

In addition to people who are seeking to augment their own education, this book may be useful to high school teachers who wish to expose their students to some aspects of the real world, and to employers who wish to use this book as professional development for their workforce. The book may also be useful to people who are transitioning into the workforce.

My background makes me something of a generalist. While I started out as a bond lawyer, I have been an executive director of a government insurance company and the administrator of health insurance regulation in the state of Hawaii. In my spare time, I also am in charge of a family business, which consists of running a small hotel operation. My varied educational background includes a bachelor of arts in English literature from Columbia University, a juris doctor from the University of California, Los Angeles, and a master's in business administration from the University of Hawaii, and I hold the Chartered Property and Casualty Underwriter designation.

Three areas that this book does not cover are science, religion, and foreign policy. I left those out partly because a short essay treatment is not really appropriate and also because these areas are not my personal strengths.

Chapter One

Division

Why do we do division? Division consists of a numerator over a line with a denominator under the line. This is otherwise known as a fraction (or a ratio), and it can be converted into a single number with decimals. We do division to find out how many units of the numerator there are for each one unit of the denominator. To take a simple example:

$$5/1$$

This means that there are five units of the numerator for each one unit of the denominator, so when we solve for the fraction and convert it to a number, the answer is 5.

To take a slightly more complicated example:

$$5/3$$

If we convert this fraction into a number with decimals, we get 1.666667. In English, we can say that there are 1.666667 units of the numerator for each 1 unit of the denominator.

That is why we do division. Addition, subtraction, and multiplication are much easier to understand and need no explanation.

Chapter Two

Economics

Economics is the study of how resources are allocated in society. There are different ways of doing that, but in the United States we use a private market system to allocate most resources. Under this system, people use their own money to buy things based on their own personal preferences. Businesspeople try to sell them things to buy, and if they are successful in doing that, then their business survives.

A **market** is composed of buyers and sellers, and the relationship between the buyers and sellers determines the price of the product or service. If you have a market with a lot of buyers and few sellers, in general the price will tend to be higher. If you have a market with few buyers and a lot of sellers, in general the price will tend to be lower. We call the buying behavior of buyers **demand** and the selling behavior of sellers **supply**. Most of economics boils down to the interplay of supply and demand. As prices go up, the demand for the product or service tends to go down. However, the sensitivity of demand to changes in price differs depending on the situation. For example, people with diabetes who need insulin to survive will buy it regardless of its price. But in general, the more competition there is between sellers, the better the overall situation is for buyers, because there is generally more choice at lower prices. As prices go up, the supply of the product or service tends to increase as sellers try to take advantage of the higher prices to increase revenues. The higher prices tend to lower demand. So a kind of balance is reached between demand and supply at any given moment. It is worth nothing that under federal antitrust law, sellers may not collude to fix prices because we want to encourage active competition based on price.

The private market economy is a demand-driven economy in that it is mainly the decisions of buyers that determine how resources are allocated. Spending by buyers, whether they are consumers or businesses, stimulates the economy. Savings by consumers or businesses generally get put into investments, where they find their way into the financing of businesses in the form of either loans or equity. But if every dollar was saved and none was spent, then the economy would not do very well, because you need spending, or demand, to drive the economy forward.

Economics is concerned with incentives for behavior. For example, in a market system, people are paid differently depending on the kinds of jobs they have and whether they are able to provide services or products that people want to buy. One of the reasons that we tolerate differences in compensation is because these differences create a strong incentive that will encourage people to work hard, be creative, take risks, and achieve. People that want to make more money will try hard to do so.

Although the basic theory suggests that the allocation of resources in a private market is basically rational, we know that sometimes people do not behave with perfect rationality because they do not have perfect foresight and sometimes because information does not spread through the market with perfect efficiency. There are limits to what people can know in a complex world. Sometimes there is a kind of herd behavior in the market which leads to speculative bubbles, for example. But, in general, we expect people to act more or less in their perceived self-interest. It was Adam Smith who first observed that this pursuit of individual self-interest could result in a better life for everyone in society through increased prosperity and division of labor, a phenomenon he called "the invisible hand."

The key to dealing with economic theory is to recognize that is it just that: theory. In real life there are situations in which the predictions of economic theory turn out to be wrong. In addition, because the economy is so complex, economic theory has proven to be very imperfect at predicting what effect certain actions with have on the overall economy. In addition, economics has not been very helpful on key issues such as how big government should get, how high taxes should get, and how high government debt should get.

It is also important to recognize the limitations of the market system. The market system will only work for you if you have ability to pay for something you want. If you have no money, you are out of luck. In addition, while the market system will react quickly to things it knows about, like changes in price, it will not react if it generally does not know something. Because information does not flow easily or quickly through the market, sometimes the market is blind to some things that are happening. In addition, one should be aware of the role of government. You need government to lay a foundation for the market system by protecting property rights and contract rights and providing basic infrastructure and security. The government should provide the public goods that everyone should be able to enjoy regardless of ability to pay. The market economy is dynamic and there are no guarantees. Many businesses go out of business and many people lose their jobs. Things are constantly changing.

In examining the workings of the market in the United States, it should be noted that not all markets are completely free. There is substantial regulation of business, particularly in some areas such as finance. In addition, we have a complex web of subsidies to business, primarily implemented through the tax code. In many areas of the economy, we are running a mixed system that is partially about free-market principles and partially about govern-mental control. There is considerable debate about the degree to which government should be involved in the market. Some people think that government can help the market do better, while oth-ers think that government involvement in the market makes both worse. In fact, some things we do are completely inconsistent with the market system. For example, when the government bails out private business, that is not the market system. Under the market system, failing business should be allowed to fail because they have outlived their usefulness, a process economist Joseph Schumpeter called "creative destruction."

Probably the greatest economist in history was Adam Smith. Smith outlined the basic workings of the market system in his book *An Inquiry into the Nature and Causes of the Wealth of Nations (1776).* The reason Smith is so great is because his methodology is entirely empirical. He makes observations about the world in painstaking detail, and from these observations he derives his theories about what is going on. Many economists do not achieve the quality of Smith because they are primarily theoreticians who are low on ac-tual data support. You can be a very smart person, but if you don't stick closely to reality and fact, you can easily end up being wrong.

Since FDR, the federal government has used the theories of economist John Maynard Keynes to stimulate the economy through higher government spending and tax cuts funded by bor-rowing long-term debt. The federal government has also enacted expensive entitlement programs that protect the needy which also involve heavy government spending. Over time, these poli-cies have left the United States with a mountain of debt and un-funded liabilities. The question is whether Keynesian policy that advocates high government spending is really sustainable over the long term. If not, then it may not be practical, despite having some theoretical merit.

Finally, in thinking about the market system, it is important to remember what a market is. A market is composed of human be-ings, and all of the limitations in the knowledge and perception of human beings can also afflict the market. No one claims that the market system is perfect or even that it can be all things to all people. However, the market system is the best mechanism we know to efficiently allocate resources and to increase wealth among people.

Chapter 3

Finance

Finance usually involves the investment of money in exchange for the possibility of making a return on that money.

There are some basic aspects of finance that one ought to know before one starts to make investments.

First, we ought to consider what a market price or market valuation is. A **market price** is the value that the market, composed of willing buyers and sellers, currently is willing to buy and sell at. But does this market price have anything to do with intrinsic value? Sometimes it does. For example, if we set a price by considering the cost to produce one unit of the product, and then add profit on top of that, the market price bears some relation to value. As another example, if the price of a piece of real estate bears some relationship to the income that the property can produce or the cost to build on that property, then the market price bears some relation to value. But sometimes market valuations can get out of whack because of price bubbles. At one time in the Netherlands, there was a craze to buy tulips, and a huge market developed in tulips where prices rose to incredible levels, in what we call a bubble. Then one day the bubble burst and the market collapsed.

We see bubbles in other areas, but the tulip example is a good one because tulips do not have much intrinsic value. The moral of the story is that you have to be careful when you look at the market-price of something, because the relationship of that price to the actual value may not be as close as you might think. In addition, market prices can be volatile.

This leads to the question of your time horizon for holding the investment. If your time horizon is short, you can expect high price volatility. Over very long periods of time, the story may be different. For example, if we examine the stock market over a fifty year period, we see a general upwards price trend. But if you look at the stock market over shorter time frames, such as five years or ten years, you see extreme price volatility, and there is no guarantee of a steadily increasing price.

Second, we ought to consider what a normal **rate of return** is. Rates of return vary as the market varies, but if someone promises a rate of return larger than 10 percent on a sustained basis, you should check it out carefully to make sure that you are not being tricked, because a normal rate of return can be even lower than 10 percent. For bonds, at the time of the writing of this book, normal rate of return might be 3 or 4 percent. If something looks too good to be true, then you have to watch out. Quite often, in order to make a higher return, you have to take on more risk. Risk means that you don't necessarily get the return. In fact, you might end up losing a lot of money. There is no guarantee when you make investments that you will make money. So you have to understand your own risk tolerances given your own financial position. My own personal viewpoint is that people who have less than $500,000 to invest should probably stick to investments that are relatively safer (and simpler to understand), such as bonds.[1]

---

1   Note that bond mutual funds carry interest rate risk, which means that as market interest rates rise, the principal value of the bond portfolio will go down. The reason is that bonds are fixed rate investments, so if the current interest rates for new bonds are higher than the rates for older bonds, the older bonds will lose value.

The reason I say that is because if you have only $500,000 to invest, then you really cannot afford to lose that money, and heavy risk taking might not be the right approach.

Third, if you do not fully understand what you are investing in, then you should beware of making the investment. Financial products can be complex, and it can be difficult to evaluate the risk of the investment. Even sophisticated investors are sometimes unable to properly evaluate the risk of investments when they are complex. So if you are going to buy something, make sure you know what you are buying.

Fourth, you ought to understand what inflation is. **Inflation** is a general decrease in the value of your currency, which means that each dollar you have has less purchasing power than it did before. Inflation generally occurs because the money supply is growing too fast relative to the goods and services produced by the economy. It should be distinguished from price increases which are the result of ordinary fluctuations in supply and demand. Inflation occurs on a marketwide basis. The reason it is important to know something about inflation when you are doing investments is that some investments hold up better under inflation than others because their prices tend to go up at the same time that inflation is happening. For example, if you hold cash, inflation will hit you harder than if you hold something, such as real estate, that tends to go up in value over a long period of time.

Fifth, one of the reasons the top income earners in America show a bigger increase in their income over time than other people is that it takes money to make money. Getting rich is about being an owner of something and making returns on your investment. At a certain point, if you are lucky, the investment return starts to have a snowballing effect because you make money on the investment and then are able to reinvest that money in new investments. If you're not on track to some kind of ownership, it is going to be difficult to really put yourself in a good position regarding saving for your children's college expenses and your own retirement. Personal property usually ends up having very little value, so if you can focus on buying investments instead of personal property, you will do better financially.

Sixth, in investing most people will follow the principle of **diversification**, which is simply the idea that you do not want all of your eggs in one basket. One of the reasons for diversification is that different types of investments perform differently in a given time frame. When corporate bonds are up, small capitalization stocks may be down, and so forth. By having diversification, you can better handle the volatility that necessarily comes from being in the investment market. Investment advisers often talk about asset allocation, which just means that you might want to set percentages on the maximum amount of money you want invested in any particular class of assets: e.g., stocks versus bonds versus real estate, etc.

Seventh, I want to address the idea that people are too stupid to invest properly. You can hear this idea when people talk about dollar cost averaging. Dollar cost averaging means that each month, you invest the same amount of money in a given investment, probably a mutual fund. The reason this is suggested is because people are too dumb to time the market properly. Along similar lines, it should be noted that Burton Malkiel wrote a book called *A Random Walk Down Wall Street* in which he proved that unmanaged index mutual funds did better than actively managed mutual funds, particularly after considering the extra fees paid for active management. There is no doubt that some people are too stupid to time the market. There is no doubt that the market is too complicated for people to predict with accuracy what is going to happen. But I personally don't tell people to dollar cost average, because to me that is like telling people that when you buy something you shouldn't consider the price. I wouldn't ever say that. I would always say that you should look for bargains when you invest. As to investing in unmanaged index mutual funds, I personally use that approach, but only because I am unwilling to put the extra time into research and monitoring that is needed with a more active stock selection strategy. That is a personal choice and you need not follow it. But if you get into active stock picking, then you really have to do your homework.

Learning finance is mostly about learning the vocabulary of finance. You don't have to be a math person to understand finance. To help you learn the vocabulary, I have created a short story that will take you through the basics of what you need to know.

Finance is using money to pay for things when we don't have enough money to pay for them by ourselves. To help us, our society has created ways for us to get money to do the things we want to do. This story is about the way we use money to accomplish goals. We will follow Brendan Smith, who is thirty years old and who wants to accomplish a lot of things. As he journeys through the world of finance, we will learn what he learns.

Brendan wants to buy a bicycle. At the nearby bicycle store, he finds one that he likes for $250. Since he has that much money in his savings account, he goes ahead and buys it. Brendan doesn't need financing because he has paid for the bicycle with cash. As long as you have enough cash, you can accomplish things without financing from other people. The way most people get their cash is by having a job that pays them a salary. Some people get cash by owning a business. Others get cash by owning income-producing assets.

The problem is that some things cost more money than you have in your savings account. Brendan also wants to buy a house to live in. The problem is that the house he wants to buy costs $300,000. Brendan looked in his savings account and found only $50,000. What is he to do? Brendan goes down to his local bank and finds out from the banker that he can borrow money from the bank to buy the house. The banker tells him this is called a **loan**. The bank will give Brendan the money to buy the house up front, and then Brendan will pay the money back to the bank over the next thirty years. Another word for a loan is **debt**, meaning that Brendan owes an obligation to the bank. Brendan also has to make a down payment of $25,000 on the loan so that the bank knows he has a stake in the property.

Now you may ask why the bank would do such a thing for Brendan. The reason the bank is willing to loan money to Brendan is that Brendan not only has to pay back what he has borrowed, but must pay an additional charge called **interest**. Interest is a fee for borrowing money. The interest rate you get depends on the bank you go to, your own creditworthiness, and what the **market** says the rate should be. Sometimes interest rates are high and sometimes they are low. In this case, the banker offers Brendan a loan at an interest rate of 7 percent annually. That means that each year, the bank is making a profit of 7 percent of the amount of the loan that hasn't been paid pack yet. In the first year, the interest on a $300,000 loan would be $21,000. Now you can see why the bank might want to make that loan to Brendan in the first place. It can make a lot of money over a thirty-year period.

Brendan has to make a payment on the loan every month. This payment is not just the payment of interest, but also a repayment of a small part of the money the bank loaned to Brendan, which is called **principal**. Each month Brendan pays a little bit of interest and little bit of principal on his loan payment. The amount of principal that is paid changes over the life of the loan, but there is a way to figure it out so that Brendan pays the same dollar amount each month for thirty years. Payment of principal and interest is called loan **amortization**. Another term for that payment is **debt service**. Brendan's loan is set up so that in the early years, most of his loan payment goes to pay interest, and then, in the later years, most of it goes to pay principal.

The bank offered Brendan a fixed rate of interest of 7 percent annually, but the bank also offers adjustable-rate loans, which change their interest rate as the market changes. If you have an adjustable-rate mortgage and the rate of interest goes up over the life of your loan, it can be rough on your pocketbook.

You may ask yourself why the bank trusts Brendan to make payments on the loan over a thirty-year period. The first thing the bank did before it gave Brendan a loan was to find out how much money he makes in his job. The bank has to make sure that

Brendan has enough income to pay for his personal expenses and to pay make the monthly loan payments. The second thing the bank does is take **security** for the loan. This means that the bank will put a mortgage on the house that Brendan buys. A **mortgage** is a document that allows the bank to sell Brendan's house if he doesn't make loan payments. If the bank sells Brendan's house, it will collect the amount of the unpaid loan if it can and give Brendan back the rest of the money. When the bank sells a mortgaged house to obtain the proceeds it is called a foreclosure.

But the bank is even more careful than that. It is worried that the house might burn down and it will be left with no security. It tells Brendan that if he wants to get a loan, he must have insurance on the house. Brendan scratches his head. "What is insurance?" he asks. The bank tells him to go talk to an insurance agent, which is a person that sells insurance.

The insurance agent explains the concept of insurance to Brendan. **Insurance** is an agreement through which an insurance company agrees to pay for your unexpected losses. With homeowner's insurance, the company will pay if the house burns down or strong winds damage the house or a whole variety of other losses occurs. Insurance is present where there is both risk transfer and risk pooling. **Risk transfer** means that Brendan, as the homeowner, is going to transfer his risk of loss to the insurance company. This simply means that if Brendan's house burns down, the insurance company will pay for the loss, not Brendan. Why would the insurance company do that for Brendan? Well, Brendan has to pay an annual **premium**, which is a fee for having insurance coverage. This is the risk pooling element of insurance. **Risk pooling** means that the insurance company will give insurance to a lot of people and collect premiums from each of those people and put them into a pool of money that can be used to pay losses. Brendan finds out that he has to pay $1,500 a year to insure his house. That may seem like a lot of money, but if Brendan's house burns down, the insurance company may have to pay him $300,000 to replace it.

This makes Brendan wonder a bit. How can the insurance company agree to pay $300,000 when it is only collecting $1,500 in premium from him? The reason is that most people insured by the insurance company don't have a loss. Only a few people each year suffer a loss on their homes. If you collect a little bit of money from a lot of people, and only a few of them suffer losses, you can cover those losses with the money you collect. This is the essence of the risk pooling mechanism. You will notice that what this means is that for a lot of people who have insurance, they pay premiums out every year and they get no money back. People who do not have losses subsidize people that do have losses.

Some people have a misunderstanding about insurance. Some people think that they pay premiums into an insurance company and it goes into a bank account that builds up over time, and that one day they collect on that amount that is built up. This is not the way that insurance works. The way insurance works is that an insurance company sets its premium prices so that it collects enough each year in total to pay that year's losses in total plus make a little bit of profit. It does not collect money to pay out in future years, although it may use some of its profit to build a cash reserve. The only reason we can even have insurance is because large losses happen infrequently and small losses happen more frequently. If it were the other way around, the premiums would be so expensive that no one could pay for them.

But Brendan, being curious, wonders whether an insurance company only gets its money through premiums. The insurance agent has an answer for him. Like most companies, the insurance company has two other ways, in addition to collecting premiums, of getting money to finance its operations. The first way is to borrow money. The insurance company can borrow money from a bank, just like Brendan does. However, unlike Brendan, the insurance company can also borrow money from the public by issuing bonds. A **bond** is merely a loan from the public to the company. Like a bank loan, the borrower, in this case the company, pays a fixed rate of interest. What is different is that the lender is not one person, but many persons from the public who are investing in the bond. The other way the insurance company can get money is by selling equity. **Equity** is an ownership interest in the company. Another name for equity is **stock**. When the public buys equity or stock, they get a piece of paper that says they own a percentage interest in the value of the company. This value of that interest can go up or it can go down. Now you should understand that it is not just insurance companies that finance themselves through stocks and bonds. Most big companies finance themselves this way, in addition to the profits they make on their business.

Brendan realizes that in some ways he is like a big corporation. Brendan is the owner of some things, but he also has some debts. That is not too different from a big insurance company that has stocks and bonds. Brendan realizes that just like a big company, he can figure out a debt-to-equity ratio. A **debt-to-equity ratio** is a comparison between the amount of debt you have and the amount of equity you have. In general, it is a good idea if the amount of debt doesn't get too big in relation to the amount of equity. The total amount of debt and equity of a corporation is equal to its total assets. **Assets** are what the corporation owns. Debt and equity of a corporation are also called the **liabilities** of the corporation, or the amounts that are owed to others. Another way to think of it is to say that the liabilities are the sources of funds and the assets are the uses of funds.

The financial diagram of a company is as follows:

Assets		Debt
		Equity

Now Brendan is pretty happy. He has a house and some insurance in case something goes wrong. The problem is that Brendan's income isn't always enough to pay for all the things he wants to buy. For example, Brendan wants to buy a big liquid crystal television for $1,000, but since he is paying on his home loan and his insurance, he doesn't have the money available. He could take money out of his savings account, but he realizes that it is good to have a small reserve for emergencies. What can he do? Brendan goes back to his bank and asks for help.

The banker tells him that they will give him a credit card and he can use that to pay for the liquid crystal television. What is a credit card? A **credit card** is a way of getting the bank to make small loans to you that you pay back fairly quickly. Brendan likes this idea, so he puts it to work right away. He goes down to the electronics store and buys a television and pays for it with his credit card. The bank pays the electronics store for the television, and now Brendan owes the money back to the bank. He doesn't have to pay it back right away, but the credit card has a high interest rate of 18 percent, so he wants to pay it back sooner rather than later. You may ask why the bank would take the risk of letting Brendan borrow money any time he wants to. The way the bank protects itself is by setting a limit on the total amount Brendan can borrow. In Brendan's case, because he is a first-time credit card borrower, his credit card limit is $5,000. Some people have much higher borrowing limits on their credit cards.

Brendan is fascinated by this world of finance that he has encountered, so he asks his banker to explain more about it. The banker explains that debt is a common financing method for the general public, corporations, and governments. The kind of debt that is used differs a little bit, however, depending on the borrower. The general public generally gets bank loans or credit cards. Corporations either get bank loans or they issue bonds to the public. Governments generally only issue bonds to the public. Equity financing through the sale of stock to the public is generally done only by corporations. If you look at the big picture, what is happening is that people or corporations with savings are putting their money into banks or stocks and bonds, and that money is being used to finance activity.

But Brendan isn't done with his banker. Brendan, as you will recall, has $25,000 in savings. He wants to know what can be done with it. There are a variety of options, his banker tells him. First,

Brendan can keep his money in his bank savings account or a certificate of deposit. If he does that, then he is loaning his money to the bank so that the bank can turn around and make loans to other people. In exchange, he gets interest. Second, Brendan can buy stock in a corporation. This can be a little bit risky because, as we saw before, the value of stock can go up or down. Third, Brendan can buy bonds issued by a corporation or by the government. This is less risky than stock, but still somewhat risky. Fourth, Brendan can buy a mutual fund. A **mutual fund** is a corporation whose sole purpose is to invest in the stocks of other corporation or the bonds of other corporations or governments. Stock mutual funds go up and down in value just as stocks do. Bond mutual funds pay interest just as bonds do. Brendan tells his banker that he will have to think about it a bit before he decides what to invest in. The banker tells Brendan that this wise and that he should never invest in anything that he does not completely understand. The banker says that there are a lot of different kinds of financial products in the market, and some are pretty complicated, so that Brendan should look before he leaps.

We have learned a lot by following Brendan on his journey through the world of finance. We have learned about banking, stocks, bonds, and insurance. But we have not asked ourselves whether all of this is a good thing. So let us examine that question. Generally, if some people have money that they are saving, it is a good thing that there is a way that they can make that money available to other people who want to use it. That way, money doesn't lay idle, but gets put to good use. The other benefit of finance is that debt allows us to spend money before we have it in hand. That is good, because by borrowing we can spend more money now than we otherwise would. Because we can do that, our economy is healthier than it might otherwise be. Of course, there is a downside in that one day that money has to be paid back. A certain amount of debt is acceptable for society, but too much can be a bad thing. Insurance is important because it stabilizes the entire market by protecting people and corporations from unexpected losses.

Chapter 4

Accounting

The most basic principle of accounting is comparing the money coming in to the money going out. I use a spreadsheet to do this for my personal finances and my family business, and just the act of keeping this kind of record puts you in the frame of mind you need to be in, in order to think intelligently about your fiscal situation. If your money coming in exceeds your money going out, that is good, because you are saving for the future. If your money coming in is less than the money going out, you are digging a hole for yourself. To keep track of your financial position, you need to understand an income statement. It is simply:

> Income
> <u>MINUS Expenses</u>
> EQUALS Net income

On my personal finance spreadsheet, I show these figures for each month, and I break down the revenues and expenses by categories so I can see where the damage is being done.

You should also be able to read a balance sheet of a company. If you are not familiar with this, it is worth knowing the accounting equation that says that ASSETS = LIABILITIES + OWNER'S EQUITY. The assets (left side of the balance sheet) are equal to the claims against the assets (right side of the balance sheet) held by the creditors and the owners. In other words, the assets are equal to the amount owed to the creditors plus the amount owned by the owners. Thus your balance sheet tells you how much of your assets are owed to others and how much of the assets are owed by yourself.

> Assets
> <u>MINUS Liabilities</u>
> EQUALS Owner's Equity
> OR
> Assets   =   Liabilities
>   PLUS Owner's Equity

What is the relationship between the income statement and the balance sheet? At the end of the period, net income from the income statement (income – expenses = net income) flows into the owner's equity on the balance sheet. Note that the value of the stock in the company often far exceeds the assets, because stock involves a prediction about the future value of the company. Note also that if you are creating a balance sheet for yourself, then owner's equity means net worth. In looking at any balance sheet, you want to make sure that the ratio of debt to owner's equity or net worth isn't too large. If debts get too large relative to what you own, the interest payments can eat you alive.

The other financial statement that you often see is the statement of cash flows. This statement will tell you where the revenues are going.

The two methods of keeping accounting records are the cash basis method and the accrual method. Under the **cash basis method**, expenses and revenues are recognized in the period (e.g., a month) in which the cash actually flows in and out of the operating account. For tax purposes, taxpayers include income when it is received and claim deductions when expenses are paid. Under the **accrual method**, expenses and revenues are recognized in the period in which they accrue, even if the cash transfer actually occurs much later. Revenue is recognized when it is earned and is realized or realizable. Expenses are recognized in the period in which the related revenues are recognized (the so-called matching principle). For tax purposes, taxpayers using the accrual method include income when it is earned and claim deductions when expenses are incurred. Most individuals use the cash basis method.

Chapter 5

Law

The first thing you need to know about law is that ignorance of the law is no excuse. That means that although the law is now so huge and complex that no one knows it all, you can still be held in violation of a law even though you never heard of it. Sorry, but we can't run our society any other way.

What are the sources of law? There are constitutions that come from political processes called constitutional conventions. There are statutes enacted by legislative bodies. And there are cases decided by judges who interpret constitutions and statutes. Judges also create the **common law**, which consists of ideas developed in cases over a long period of time. The law is primarily about policy and governance. We don't fully enforce morality through the law, although you can see elements of morality in things like the criminal law.

Legal reasoning is a process by which we navigate between the law, which is usually a rule, and the facts of the case. Sometimes it is easy to see that the law has been violated, but sometimes it is not clear. Navigating between the law and the facts is the job of the judge. You will find that normally what is most important in a case is not knowing the law, but knowing the facts. The facts are what drive the outcome.

Lawyers will try to argue one side of the case versus another. In our adversarial system of justice, a lawyer will tell a very one-sided story on behalf of his client and leave it to the judge to determine the truth. In the argument, a lawyer will try to draw analogies between prior cases that favor his client and the current case. To defeat the other lawyer, he will then draw distinctions between prior cases that are favorable to his opponents and the current case. It is a complex process. There can be a lot of grey area in the law, because sometimes the words that make up the law do not fit that well on the facts of a given cases. Although lawyers will give opinions on the legality of certain actions to guide their clients, you don't really know if the law is being violated until a judge makes a decision that the law has been violated. Lawyers have different views about the law, and some are willing to stretch the law further than others. But you always have to be a little careful because if you stretch the law too far, sometimes you break it. A lot of times, it is a good idea to stand back from the line a little bit just to be safe.

In a court, all facts must be proved by evidence, and there are complicated rules associated with that. Upon appeal, the reviewing court will normally review errors of law and not retry the underlying facts. The vast majority of cases are settled out of court, and there is nothing inherently wrong with that. A lot can go wrong when you go to trial.

Some lawsuits are reserved to the government to prosecute, while most lawsuits can be litigated by private attorneys.

People are often protected from lawsuits with **liability insurance**. This means that if they get sued, the insurance company will hire a lawyer to put up a defense. Normally, the lawyer is suing to get money out of the insurance company, not you. But if you don't have liability insurance, or the liability is something that is not covered by the insurance, or the damages exceed what the insurance will pay, then you may have to pay with your own assets. It is a good idea to have liability insurance, particularly if you own a business, because any and all manner of lawsuits can be filed. The only thing a lawyer has to be able to show when he files a lawsuit is that he has a good-faith argument under the law. Well, the good faith/bad faith standard is a very low standard. In our family business, we got sued once because someone claimed to have hurt her hand while getting a soda out of the soda machine that was located on the premises. That should give you some idea of what lawyers can throw at you.

In addition to filing lawsuits, lawyers also prepare legal documents and give advice on how to act in a way that complies with the law.

The **rule of law** is the idea that a civilization is best served when there is a system in which the law is supreme, rather than the whim or mood of any man or men. The law protects people from government and from each other and creates order and predictability. It also means that no one is above the law. John Adams, our second president, talked about a republic being a nation of laws and not of men. Aristotle said that "the rule of law is better than that of any individual." The rule of law is important because people need to be able to plan their affairs in accordance with established, stable rules of the game.

A **contract** is an agreement, usually between two parties, in which each party agrees to do something it didn't otherwise have to do. Having a promise on each side of the agreement is called **consideration**. Normally contracts are formed when someone makes an offer and another person accepts that offer. Oral promises are enforceable because you only need a written agreement when you are dealing in land or if the contract cannot be performed within one year. The vast majority of contracts are not negotiated because one party has all the power and the other party has none. Generally, contract negotiation only occurs between parties of equal bargaining power. If you need to do the transaction more than the other guy does, then he is in a superior bargaining position, particularly if you are under some time pressure. Another rule of thumb is the golden rule that "he who has the gold makes the rules." If I am in a situation where I know that I have no negotiating position, then I normally just sign the documents that are presented to me. If I don't want to do the deal because of the contract terms, then I should just walk away from the whole thing.

If you are called to testify in a hearing, you have to be a little careful, because lawyers can make a lot of trouble if you don't testify the right way. Of course, the whole point is that you are speaking under oath and so you must tell the truth. But there is still a right way and a wrong way to go about telling the truth, and you certainly don't want to just run off at the mouth and go all over the place. Here are five rules of thumb that are useful to remember when testifying:[2]

a. Make sure you understand the question before answering.
b. Think of the answer in your head before you speak, at least to the extent it makes sense to do that.
c. Answer the question.
d. Don't help the lawyer with his question, for example, by asking, "Are you asking me X?" The silence belongs to the lawyer.
e. When done with the answer, be silent. Don't volunteer information.

If you follow these simple rules, you can testify with some confidence that you won't get yourself into too much trouble.

The best way to avoid legal problems is not a matter of knowing the law, but rather a matter of knowing who to do business with. If you do business with reputable, professional people, you will have fewer problems that can turn into legal matters. Being a smart market player will beat legal knowledge any day of the week. If you do file a lawsuit, it is a good idea to have the lawyer represent you on a **contingency basis** so that you only end up paying the lawyer if you win the case. There is enough uncertainty about whether a case will be decided in your favor by the judge that it generally

---

2   These rules of thumb came from a fine practicing litigator named Dianne Brookins, Esq.

isn't a good idea to promise to pay hourly fees even if you lose, because these fees can be substantial. Being angry or righteous about something isn't a good reason to make a foolish financial decision. The good thing about a contingency fee is that it brings the lawyer's interests into complete alignment with your interests as the client. When the lawyer is billing hours, there is a built in conflict of interest, because the longer he takes, the more money he makes off of you.

Finally, when looking for a lawyer, try to remember that lawyers are not all created equal. Going to law school and passing a bar examination might mean that you're not a moron, but it doesn't necessarily make you a genius. Check out the rankings of law schools to get a sense of which lawyers might be in the top academic range. The best way to find lawyers is by word of mouth. You are looking for someone with expertise in the area that is the subject of your lawsuit, and people will have good things to say about lawyers who did a good job for them previously. But if you just go looking in the Yellow Pages or use a bar referral service, you are really rolling the dice.

Chapter 6

Civics

It is a good idea to learn about the government, because the government makes the rules that we have to live by and makes important policy decisions that affect all of us. We need a government to have an orderly society where people get along with each other. When a government is run right, it can also create the right conditions for people to do business with each other. The United States is a **democracy**, which means that the power to govern is derived from the consent of the people who are governed. Democracy is based on the idea that people have some basic rights as human beings that are independent of the scheme of governance.

In the United States, there are three levels of government. On the top is the federal government, which governs the entire United States. In the middle are the fifty separate state governments, each of which governs a single state. On the bottom are local governments, which generally cover the cities and counties within a state.

The United States is a country that believes in the rule of law. The **rule of law** means that we do things according to written rules that have been enacted by the government. The highest law in the

United States is the U.S. Constitution. A constitution is a document that sets forth the most important rules for a society. The U.S. Constitution does two basic things: it sets up the government; and it protects citizens from the government. Each state also has a state constitution.

According to the U.S. Constitution and every single state constitution, there are three branches of government: the executive branch, the legislative branch, and the judicial branch. These branches are separate and have equal power and importance. The **legislative branch** makes the laws. The **executive branch** carries out the laws. The **judicial branch** resolves disputes under the law and interprets the law. The three branches of government exist at the top two levels of government: federal and state. The local governments have an executive branch and legislative branch, but rely on the state courts or local courts to resolve disputes.

You may ask yourself why there should be three separate branches of government. The reason is that the people that set up the United States did not want any one person or branch to have too much power. By dividing the government into separate branches, they made each branch provide **checks and balances** on the other branches.

You may also ask yourself why there should be three levels of government—federal, state, and local. The reason is that the people that set up the United States did not want the national federal government to have too much power. They wanted individual states to have some power also, so they could make decisions for themselves. The benefit of doing it that way is that sometimes one size does not fit all, and it is good to let the fifty states come up with their own solutions. The other benefit is that state and local governments may be closer to the people than a national federal government located far away in Washington, D.C.

The system we use, in which the federal and state governments share power, is called **federalism**. Federal law is supreme over state law. Federal law often covers different topics than state law because federal law can only be within the powers given to the federal government by the U.S. Constitution. Powers not given by the Constitution to the federal government are reserved to the states and the people. For example, states have a police power to enforce health, safety and welfare that the federal government does not.

Someone has to run the executive branch. At the federal level, that person is the president of the United States. At the state level, that person is the governor of the State. At the local level, that person is usually the mayor of a city.

Someone has to run the legislative branch. At the federal level, this is called the United States Congress. At the state level, this is called a state legislature or general assembly. At the local level, this is called a city council. In both the federal and state legislatures, there are two parts to the legislature: a senate and a house of representatives.[3] Laws are voted on separately in each part of the legislature. City councils generally only have a few members, and they all vote on laws as part of one group.

To get the job of running the executive branch or legislative branch, a person has to run for election. That means that the public must cast votes to put him in office. Each person has one vote for each office. This system is called **representative democracy**, because we, the people, elect people to represent us in government. We do not ourselves make the decisions about what the government does. We leave those decisions to our elected representatives. A person elected to a political office is only elected for a specified period of time, called a **term of office**. Terms of office vary—for example, the president serves a four-year term, U.S. senators serve six-year terms, and members of the U.S. House of Representatives serve two-year terms. When the term is over, there is another election and a new person can try to become elected. By having limited terms, we have a chance to make the government respect the wishes of the voters.

---

3   The one exception is Nebraska, which is the only U.S. state with a unicameral (one house) legislature.

In order to get elected, a person mostly needs votes, but candidates also need money, because it takes money to run a political campaign. People and businesses and other organizations can contribute money to help people they like get elected. This can give people and groups who are able to contribute a lot of money some influence over elected officials. This problem is greater when someone is running for a national or statewide election, because it is expensive to buy advertising time on television and radio. Many complain about the power that businesses have in government. No doubt business should have some kind of a voice due to its importance in the economy, but the question is whether it now has too much of a voice.

A word should be said about the difference between a house of representatives and a senate. In the U.S. Congress, there are fewer senators than representatives. There are only two senators for each state. A small state, such as Hawaii, may have only two representatives, but a larger state, such as California, has fifty-three representatives because representation is based on the number of people in the state. There are a total of 435 representatives in the Congress and only one hundred senators. Having fewer people in the Senate means that each senator has more power than a representative would. Because representatives are elected to Congress every two years, but senators every six years, representatives are tied more closely to the will of the voting public than senators.

The press is not part of government, but it plays an important role in our system by reporting on what the government does. If the press does a poor job of reporting on the government, how can people vote intelligently?

To get the job of being a judge in the judicial system, we use different approaches at different levels. At the federal level, the judges are appointed by the president of United States and confirmed by the Senate. Some states use a similar system and have judges appointed by the governor of the state and confirmed by the state senate. Other states have their judges elected by the voters.

The executive branch is divided up into a number of agencies, each of which has different areas of responsibility.

The judicial branch is divided into lower courts that hear cases and higher courts that decide whether the lower courts made the right decision based on the law. Generally, federal courts hear cases involving federal law or disputes between citizens of different states. State courts generally hear cases involving state law and disputes that occur entirely within a given state. At the very top of the federal court system is the U.S. Supreme Court. At the very top of a state court system is the state supreme court. But since cases can go from a state supreme court to the U.S. Supreme Court, the U.S. Supreme Court is really the highest court in the country. You should note that if the judicial branch decides your case against you, there is no point going to the executive branch for additional help, because the judicial branch is the end of the line in terms of interpretation of law. If you want to get the law changed, then you go to the legislative branch, but the change of law is not going to be retroactive and help a past situation.

The government does many things. Some of those things are vital for our society and for running a business. For example, governments are responsible for building roads and highways. Imagine trying to run a business without roads. How would the customers come to your place of business? How would the business send goods to the customers? As another example, governments generally control the water supply and provide sewage management and waste management. The government also provides security, both in the form of a national military that defends the country from enemies around the world and local police forces that defends citizens from the criminals that live among us. To run a business without basic security would be hard.

In the United States, most people do not work for the government. Most people work for a private business that makes money. Businesses make money by selling goods or services to people in exchange for money. Where there are buyers and sellers trading goods or services for money, we call this a **market**. The government can help a market by making and enforcing laws that protect private property rights. The reason for this is clear. If someone could take away your money, why would you become a businessman and work hard to earn money? The government can also help a market by enforcing laws that make people live up to their business agreements, otherwise known as **contracts**. This helps the market by making sure that if someone agrees to sell you a good or service for money, he has to do that. Similarly, if you agree to sell someone a good or service for money, and you do what you said you were going to do, then the buyer has to pay you the money. There are other laws that can help the market. For example, we have laws called **antitrust laws** which make it illegal for businesses to get together and set prices. We think a market works better if a business sets prices only for itself and competes with other businesses for customers. We also have laws that allow us to punish people by putting them in jail if they commit fraud. A **fraud** happens when someone promises to sell you a good or service, takes your money, and then doesn't do what he promised to do.

Most of the other laws we have are designed to protect us from the harmful actions of others. For example, killing someone or stealing someone's money or property is illegal. But we also have rules for some businesses so that they do not harm consumers or create too much pollution. We make these laws because we do not think the market is completely able to police itself.

Although we have many laws in the United States, we generally encourage people and businesses to act with freedom, because we believe free choice leads to the best results. In history there have been some societies that have tried to tell people and businesses what to do, and things did not work out very well for people. The former Soviet Union is a good example of this.

The United States Constitution covers a lot of topics, but there are a few that are important for every citizen to know.

The Constitution gives the federal government responsibility for providing for a common defense. That is why we have a U.S.

military to protect us. The Congress has the power to declare war, but once war is declared, the president makes the military decisions as the commander in chief. You will note that this puts civilian authorities in charge of the military.

The Constitution puts limits on the government's ability to interfere with its citizens. For example, people have the right under the First Amendment to free speech. This right is important in a representative democracy because there needs to be the free exchange of ideas before the government makes laws. This right is also important because it helps to protect each citizen against government power. If you want to protect your right to own property, for example, it is good to be able to speak out against the government if it tries to take your property away. Finally, it is important for the press to be able to exercise free speech so that it can report to the citizens about what is going on in their government. You should be aware that the right of free speech is not absolute. For example, you cannot tell lies about your fellow citizens that make them look bad, and you cannot encourage people to commit violence or break the law.

The First Amendment also says that the government may not establish a religion or make laws prohibiting the free exercise of religion. The reason the people that created the country did that was to allow for freedom of religion. They knew that if the government established an official religion, some religious groups would get persecuted by the government and other religious groups. So under the First Amendment, we are not allowed to create a theocracy.[4]

An important right under the Fifth Amendment is the right of due process. This means that before the government takes away your life, liberty, or property, you are entitled to notice that

---

4   The Gospels are not about theocracy either. The life and times of Jesus Christ are not about the exercise of government power. That is why he says "My kingdom is not of this world" and "Render unto Caesar what is Caesar's, and unto God what is God's."

it wanted to do that and a hearing where you can tell your side of the story to a judge.

An important right under the Fourth Amendment is the right to be free from unreasonable searches and seizures by the government. The government can search your house or car, but it has to have a good reason for doing it, and often it needs the permission of a judge before it can act.

Under the Constitution and the Sixth and Seventh amendments, if you are the target of a lawsuit by the government or another citizen, you have the right to a trial by a jury of your peers. You also have the right to confront the witnesses against you and to compel people to testify on your side of the case.

You will notice that these important rights under the Constitution are about the relationship of the government to you as a private citizen, and not about your relationship to other private citizens. The Constitution is also not involved in your dealings with a private business. The Constitution is not involved in how a business deals with its workers. There must be government action for the Constitution to be involved.

The Fourteenth Amendment of the Constitution makes these rights that we have been talking about something that the state governments must also respect.

The government cannot do anything unless the law says it can do that thing. In private life, a person or a business can do anything unless the law says that it cannot do that thing. That means that the government has less freedom of action than people and business in private life. For those that fear government power and the harm it can do to people if it falls into the wrong hands, this limitation is very important.

If you get involved in public policy by advocating for things that a legislature should enact into law, it is important to remember that you have to write laws for planet Earth, not planet Zetar. That means that you have to be realistic about the world and the way things work, and particularly you have to be realistic about human nature. Legislation that does not pay heed to reality generally does not work well when it is implemented. Also, before advocating public policy, you should consider the context of where we have been, where we are, and where we are headed. If you don't understand the historical contexts and the future trends, it is easy to make a public policy blunder.

Democracy as practiced in the United States may not work everywhere. American democracy gives people a great deal of freedom, and in order for that to work, the people who are governed must have a high level of ethics. You also need people who have enough education and intelligence to exercise their democratic rights in a smart way. You also need people who are willing to cooperate and who can subordinate their own desires to the will of the majority as expressed in law.

To understand the spirit behind the American experiment, one should consult the Declaration of Independence (1776) which says that "We hold these truths to be self-evident, that all men are created equal, that they are endowed by their Creator with certain unalienable rights, that among these are life, liberty and the pursuit of happiness." The statement shows that the Founding Fathers believed that basic human rights exist prior to any government. Because the basic right of liberty comes from God, government should not exercise power in a way that destroys that right. It should also be noted that the formulation "life, liberty and the pursuit of happiness" has its origins in John Locke's formulation "life, liberty and property" from the *Second Treatise of Civil Government* (1690). The Founding Fathers saw property ownership as a centerpiece of the republic that they were creating.

Chapter 7

Critical Thinking

Underlying any decision is a basic need to ascertain the relevant facts correctly. You need to understand the real world if your decision making is going to be successful. Understanding the real world requires critical thinking.

All other things being equal, a more realistic person will beat a less realistic person most of the time. While it is true that optimists sometimes find success because they follow their dreams and take risks, it is equally true that many people make mistakes in life because they do not see the world around them clearly. To do that, one needs to be able to distinguish fact from opinion.

A **fact** is something that is known to be true. An **opinion** is a viewpoint that may or may not be true, but is debatable. Anyone looking at those two definitions will realize right away that this difference between a fact and an opinion is not a matter of black versus white, but rather shades of grey.

The first concept to know is called **observational bias**. When people in the days before Christopher Columbus thought that the world was flat, it was simply because it looked that way from where they were standing. When the NASA astronauts stood on the moon and looked back at the Earth, it looked like a ball and they knew it was not flat. A simpler example is the way a clock looks when you look at its face and see the time elements. If you turn the clock to the side, it looks very different. Almost every observation we make about the world is from our point of view. That can make a big difference in what facts we think we see.

From law or science, we can examine the role of proof in determining whether something is a fact. Some things are provably true, such as our example of the Earth being shaped like a ball. Other things may be true, but are not provable. For example, if you think someone is greedy, you may have some evidence that suggest that, but depending on the quantity of proof that we require for a conclusion and the quality of the proof you have, it may not be provably true. It can be hard to prove that someone has a characteristic, because we are talking about something that is inside their head or heart, and that is a place that no one can go. Similarly, some things are provably false, such as the notion that pink unicorns roam the planet. Other things may be false, but not provably so. For example, if someone accuses me of being unfair, I might be able to cite a few examples of cases where I had acted fairly, but I cannot really disprove the accusation, because the proof would be very complex and because the issue of unfairness is a subjective one in the first place.

The Greeks created an area of study and philosophizing called **epistemology**, which tries to find a theory of knowledge and asks, how do we know what we think we know? At the most fundamental level, we observe with our eyes and hear with our ears. This is where observational bias comes in. We see and talk to people, we watch the television, we read. Whenever we do those things, we must consider the reliability of the source of the information. How does the person speaking or writing know what he is talking about? If that person we are listening to used a source, how did that source come to know what he thought he knew? When we think about knowledge in this way, it becomes a chain of uncertainty. It is worth noting that nobody knows everything. Everyone bases his knowledge on a combination of experience plus assumptions about things they know less about. There is nothing inherently wrong with this, but it is just important to recognize it when you are considering the reliability of any source of information.

How then do we resolve this uncertainty? One way is to use multiple sources of information and see if the information agrees. There are often two sides to any issue, so it makes sense to collect information on both sides of the argument. Another way is to use reason to see if what someone is saying makes logical or practical sense. But there are many issues on which we never really have total certainty. That is the point. You have to know what you know and know what you don't know. Too many people run around being certain of things when they just don't know what they are talking about. Everyone would be better off if we all carried around a little doubt in our pockets.

No discussion of epistemology would be complete without a discussion of the dangers of generalization, extrapolation, and analogy. We will take each in turn.

If I have one date with a woman and it turns out badly, it would be a mistake to assume that all future dates with any women would turn out badly. They might, but they might not. Our society has gotten to a point where we discourage discrimination against people on the basis of race, gender, sexual orientation, and religion. Discrimination is often, although not always, based on an experience with a few people that is then generally applied to all people of that category. In fact, all people are different on an individual level, so this kind of **generalization** from the one to the many is not a reliable methodology.

Extrapolation occurs when we take a set of facts from the past and project forward into a prediction about the future. For example, an insurance company might look to the past year's loss claims and project forward into the next year that the claims might be about the same. The more data you have, the more reliable your extrapolation will tend to be. But the further out into the future you extrapolate, the less reliable the extrapolation becomes. In addition, while the past can be useful in predicting the future, it often does not predict the future because things change and the unexpected can happen. Extrapolation is really a prediction based on some data. Sometimes we make predictions without a lot of data. Of course, that is terribly risky, but when navigating through life it is sometimes unavoidable. Pessimists tend to be more accurate in predicting the future than optimists, but you can't succeed unless you try in the first place, and optimists are probably better than pessimists at taking the kinds of risks one has to take in order to succeed. The point to take away is that because prediction is about the future, the facts are not yet known. Some facts will persist from the past into the future, but not all. The world is constantly changing.

We also need to consider the difference between **correlation** and **causation**. Two data sets may be correlated because there is a causal relation between the two. For example, when interest rates rise, automobile sales decline because many automobiles are sold on the basis of a loan which carries an interest rate. However, not all correlations have a causal relation. For example, two races may have different average SAT scores, but that does not mean that race causes the different scores, because other factors could be the cause, including socioeconomic factors. Indeed, those socioeconomic factors could be caused by race or by something entirely different. The point is that to jump to a conclusion about causation just because you see a correlation of data is not a reliable methodology.

Analogies are used to find similarities between things, but one must be cautious, because very few things or cases are exactly the same when you drill down into all the details. We often argue that this case is like another case, but one can often shoot holes in that kind of argument. Apples are not the same thing as oranges, despite certain similarities.

What is the simple version of this entire chapter? Four principles: Don't believe everything you hear. Check your facts. Don't assume anything. Find out more.

Finally, we should not forget the words of former Secretary of Defense Donald Rumsfeld, who said: "There are known knowns. There are things we know that we know. There are known unknowns. That is to say, there are things that we now know we don't know. But there are also unknown unknowns. There are things we do not know we don't know." That was a very fine statement of the limitations of human knowledge. The fact is, sometimes you are operating in a situation where you are taking your best guess at what is the right course of action, but in reality you don't know what you are doing, because not everything is knowable.

Chapter 8

Decision Making

Decision making comes more easily to some people than others. I happen to be a very fast decision maker. Indeed, I got myself into trouble early on in life because I was too quick to make a decision. In other words, I decided without much thought. Because we have to make so many decisions in life, big and small, it makes sense to spend a little time examining some basic decision-making techniques.

The most basic decision-making technique is the use of **pro and con analysis**. You simply make a list of the things that are good about the decision and a list of the things that are bad about the decision and then compare the two lists. This is a good method, because almost all decisions involve trade-offs in which you have to give up something in order to gain something else.

Another decision-making technique is **issue spotting**. This is the development of a list of issues or questions that must be answered before the decision can be made. This is a good method, because almost all decisions are made in a situation where knowledge about what is going to happen is imperfect and there is uncertainty.

Another decision-making technique is to develop a list of all the alternative decisions and the possible outcomes. Of course, this can get complicated, but it will help to make sure you have not overlooked a better path.

In making a decision, one should decide how much diligence needs to be done. Some decisions can be made with very little diligence, while others require extensive diligence. Diligence can involve research, data collection, talking to people, asking for formal written recommendations, or doing some of the decision-making techniques already talked about. Of course, it makes sense to separate fast decisions from slow decisions and important decisions from unimportant decisions, because you cannot apply extensive diligence to everything you decide or nothing is going to get done in a timely fashion.

Sometimes it is a good idea to write down your thinking when making a decision. The reason is that when you write, you are forced to fully articulate your ideas, and you can set the document aside for a period of time and check it later to see if it makes sense. Some people like to decide fast "on their gut" or "off the top of their heads," but that can be dangerous if you are not that smart or if your past experience does not apply to the current or future situation about which you are making a decision. A middle ground might be to think fast, write it down, then hold off for a while and take a look at your writing later. There is some danger in forming judgments too quickly simply because at that stage, you might not have as much information as is advisable to have when deciding.

Using expert opinion can be helpful, particularly in areas where you are not expert, but you should be aware that some studies show that experts are no better than laypersons at predicting the future.

No matter what you decide and how you decide, there is always some unintended consequence that you haven't foreseen. We call this **the law of unintended consequences**, and it is unavoidable.

In making decisions, we have to watch out for the fact that we are human beings and we have weaknesses that cause us to make errors. The list to watch out for is simple:

Bias
Irrationality
Ignorance
Pride/overconfidence
Delusion or denial
Reduction/oversimplification

We humans just don't think straight all the time, and when we make decisions we have to check ourselves for these issues.

In my opinion, high-level thinking is simple, not complex. A good example of that was Bill Gates's vision for Microsoft when he said, "A computer on every desktop in the world." If you are going to follow any rule in life, follow the KISS rule: "Keep it simple, stupid."

A lot of what I have talked about in this chapter boils down to the simple idea that decision making involves a process. In many instances in business and government, we actually create a process where decisions will go through various committees or important people, and we hope that by going through some kind of process, we will get a better decision. President John F. Kennedy was famous for creating a special decision-making process to handle the Cuban Missile Crisis where he had some people argue each side of the case while others played devil's advocate. Process is not a guarantee that you make the right decision, but it can help.

In general, in making decisions it helps to be **empirical**. That means going on facts instead of on theories. There are many ideas that sound nice on paper, but which turn into disasters when you try implement them in the real world. Staying empirical is a way to keep in touch with reality while making decisions. I have a personal view that the empirical mind is superior to the theoretical mind precisely because the empirical mind tends to make fewer mistakes.

Chapter 9

Business and the Business Environment

Conceptually, business is simple. You try to sell a product or service that people want to buy at a price that they are able to afford and are willing to pay. You need to find a way to let people know about your product or service. In running the business, you want revenues to exceed expenses. In general, you try to maximize revenues. But at all times, you have to understand your customer and what his needs and wants are or could become. Businesses that do not change as demand changes may not survive over the long term.

In the final analysis, business is about creating value for people. The old sayings that you should "find a need and fill it" or "build a better mousetrap" are pretty accurate. There is a creative aspect to business. There is a problem-solving aspect to it. Business is a kind of public service with just as much moral worth as any kind of government service, because to make money you have to help people in some way. Doing well in business is not just about having the right idea, however; it is about having the right execution of the right idea. People expect a certain quality, and if you don't provide it, you will eventually lose out to your competitors. Although business may be simple conceptually, it can be difficult to achieve the right level of execution. Nothing is easy.

Sometimes in running a business you find you have to cut costs, but you don't want to cut costs so much that you seriously damage the quality of the product or service that you are selling. If you are running a business, you ought to sample the products you are selling. My secretary once bought me a recording machine that had keys labeled "Talk" and "Listen" instead of "Record" and "Play." To me that is an example of top management being completely out of touch with its own products. Be empirical. Go out and kick the tires. Of course, the other question in this case about delegation is why I let my secretary buy a tape recorder for me instead of buying one for myself.

Business operates in the market system, which is a dynamic, rough-and-tumble system, so any businessman has to keep an eye on the environment he is operating in and try to figure out what the future might hold. According to the Small Business Administration, 50 percent of small businesses fail within the first five years. Probably some of that failure rate has to do with not being realistic about the feasibility of the business in the first place. If you're thinking of starting a business, it is a good idea to get feedback on the feasibility of the idea from someone whose judgment you trust. If you rely on outside funding, like a bank loan, that kind of outside evaluation of your business plan will happen as a matter of course. To be good at running a business, you have to have a sense of what is going to work as a practical matter in the real world. Fundamentally, you have to understand the target market for your product or service. What is really going to get your potential customers to engage in buying behavior? Even if you offer people a solution to a particular problem that they have or otherwise create value for them, getting them to the point of spending money is the key step in the process. It's not that easy to get people to part with money.

The organizational structure of a business and the financial incentives that are put in place for the employees need to be aligned with the larger strategic goals of the business. In addition, ideas should be allowed to filter up through the organization from the bottom, where the people are the closest to the day-to-day operations, so that you are not only relying on ideas flowing downward from top management.

Business does not occur in a vacuum. If you compare countries around the world, it becomes clear that having the right kind of government is essential for a successful business climate. So what should businesses expect from their government?

A business should expect a government to provide basic security and infrastructure and to enforce property rights, including intellectual property, and contract rights. Without these basics, business will have a hard time. A business has a right to expect a level playing field so that competition is fair, including enforcement of antitrust laws. A business has a right to expect government not to be corrupt and not to engage in the kind of crony capitalism where government picks winners and losers. A business needs statutes to enable the creation and operation of the business entity, such as corporations and partnerships. A business needs a relatively low and stable tax environment in which to operate. A business needs to have an efficient way to enter the market (licensing) and an efficient way to exit the market (bankruptcy). A business needs a general environment that can attract workers to the business, such as affordable housing and decent education for the children of the workers. A business also needs a regulatory environment that is not excessively onerous. A business needs access to financial capital, and although this should generally not come from the government, the government plays a role in creating a stable, robust financial system. A business needs to have access to workers that have had enough quality education to do their jobs well. It helps to have rules of the road that are relatively stable and which are not constantly changing. The point is that when starting a business, you need to take a look first at the environment that your business is going to be located in.

Being successful in business requires risk taking and a certain stubbornness that says "I will not quit trying no matter what happens." Fortunately, we have some mechanisms that are designed to encourage risk taking. Corporation and bankruptcy laws can allow you to wind up a failed business without excessive personal liability. In addition we have safety nets for low-income people that can catch you when you fall. The trick is being careful about pouring your own money into a business. The purpose of the business is for you to make money, not for you to run up a huge pile of personal expenses. In the end, business success boils down to hard work, good judgment, and some luck.

My favorite example of a business was a Vietnamese immigrant to the United States who invented a new type of board that cats like to scratch their claws on. He was making millions on it. In other words, this guy got rich because he spent his time thinking about how to improve the life of a cat. That's business in a nutshell.

Bibliography for Chapter 9

Baumol, W. J., R. E. Litan, and L. J. Schramm. *Good Capitalism, Bad Capitalism, and the Economics of Growth and Prosperity.* New Haven, CT: Yale University Press, 2007.

Chapter 10

The Partisan Divide

The United States electorate is divided between liberals, conservatives, and those in the middle. Given that the American government was meant to solve problems through compromise and bipartisanship, it is worth taking a moment to consider what the key differences between liberals and conservatives are. By this I don't mean to contrast every policy position, but to contrast the differences in worldviews that underlie those policy positions. Now, of course, making generalizations in this way means that my statements may not be applicable in every case. We also know that people are complex in their thinking and a single person can be all over the political map, depending on the issue that he is considering. But because the liberal mind and the conservative mind are so fundamentally different, it is profitable to highlight these differences.

Liberals tend to focus on issues of fairness and equity. The premise they have is that all people are human beings and, as such, are entitled to fair and equitable treatment. They not only want to see equality of opportunity, they want to see equality of outcome. **Conservatives** also believe in basic human rights, but they draw the circle of those rights more narrowly. To a conservative, you should definitely have equality under the law, but no one is entitled to equality of outcomes. Although conservatives believe in equality of opportunity, it is a different kind of belief than that held by liberals. To a conservative, a level playing field means a level playing field. To a liberal, differences in people's environments and heredity create inequalities that need to be remedied by outside action. To a conservative, differences in people's environment and heredity are not things that can or should be remedied. In other words, a conservative would say that things are fair as long as everyone has access to the same education system. A liberal would say that a child with poor parents is disadvantaged and that there is no real equality of opportunity.

Conservatives emphasize personal responsibility and freedom of choice. Liberals accept these elements, but they also look at the impact of environment and heredity and the role these have in shaping behavior. To a conservative, if you make a dumb choice and end up in trouble, it is your own fault. To a liberal, it may not be someone's fault if they were born stupid or had bad parents. That is why conservatives tend to have less sympathy for the poor than liberals tend to have. To a conservative, if you are poor because you are dumb, then it is your own fault. To a liberal, many people just don't have it within them to be rich and that lack of capacity is not their fault. Liberals don't like the idea of people suffering bad consequences if they are not guilty of some fault. In this respect, the liberal perspective takes the legal perspective and applies it beyond the legal realm. Conservatives take a broad view that suggests that your situation is primarily the result of your own choices and abilitites.

Conservatives are always thinking about incentives for behavior and the bottom line. Liberals are more concerned with matters of principle, like fairness. Conservatives are willing to tolerate unfairness in order to preserve the kind of incentives for behavior that they think lead to desirable consequences. To a liberal, it is not fair that a child who was brought into the U.S. illegally by his parents cannot become a citizen. To a conservative, granting citizenship in that situation increases the incentive for illegal immigration to occur in the first place.

Conservatives are distrustful of government solutions, while liberals tend to embrace government solutions. Conservatives want a limited government; liberals like a big government. Conservatives and liberals generally support the market system, but while conservatives have faith that the market system can solve everything important, liberals tend to believe that the market system only works up to a point. Liberals think the market has flaws and can lead to excesses and bad consequences. The conservative critique of big government is that it harms the economy and the market system through excessive taxation, excessive business regulation, and redistribution of income schemes that remove the incentive to work hard.

Both liberals and conservatives will use government and the law to achieve control over behavior that they don't like, but in some cases the type of behavior that they don't like differs.

Liberals tend to see all the people in society as part of an extended family where we each bear responsibility for the welfare of the others. It is a collectivist vision that holds that no one should be left too far behind. Conservatives take a much more individualistic view that holds that everyone must take care of himself or herself and that people are on their own. F. A. Hayek has made the point that the collectivist vision often results in a loss of freedom as government tries to force equity into the system.

Actor Rob Lowe described liberals as proceeding from empathy and conservatives as proceeding from reason. That is a generalization, but it does a pretty good job of summarizing at a high level the different perspectives of the two sides. I would add that I think liberals understand the idea of moral luck, which is that what happens to you in life is partly the result of luck and not of your own doing. For a liberal, it makes sense to show concern for people who, through no fault of their own, have bad luck. Conservatives have less of a concern because "that's life." Conservatives believe that if you have been dealt a poor hand, then you simply have to work harder to overcome your challenges. Liberals are idealistic, and they tend to see the cup as half empty and the world as being in need of improvement. Conservatives tend to be accepting of the world as it is, even with all of its flaws. Liberals tend to be more utopian than conservatives.

Liberals support labor unions, while conservatives have an affinity for business owners. Both conservatives and liberals believe in military defense spending, but there is a disagreement about the size of that spending and the degree to which military intervention is advisable. There are some anti-war and pro-isolationism factions on both the liberal and conservatives side. Liberals are strict about the idea that government should be stripped of religion, while conservatives defend the expression of religion in the public sphere. Liberals sometimes take the view that good Christian works should be accomplished through the government, while conservatives tend to think Christian works are for individuals and charitable or religious organizations to accomplish. Liberals are concerned about the environment, while conservatives believe the environment is a lower priority than jobs and economic productivity. Conservatives tend to be mistrustful of the idea that lawyers and lawsuits make things better, while liberals tend to embrace the rights vindication that lawyers achieve.

Liberals criticize conservatives as being mean, and they sometimes are, or at least they are unempathetic. On the other side of the coin, British Prime Minister Margaret Thatcher said of socialists that "they always run out of other people's money," and this remains a trenchant critique of the liberal approach to government.

The ideological/philosophical divide between liberals and conservatives can become a problem when people start to depart from empirical or historical reality and start making arguments that are largely based on a faith in a worldview. As Daniel Patrick Moynihan put it, "You are entitled to your own opinions, but you are not entitled to your own facts." The political system in this country was designed to solve problems through compromise. Indeed, you cannot solve the really big problems without compromise. Ideology can sometimes get in the way of compromise.[5] With a divided country, consensus can be hard to find. But in the end, we will be a stronger nation if we can work together.

---

5   Compromise is not always a good thing. If someone is absolutely wrong, then they should be opposed absolutely. The point is that people can reasonably differ on policy and the number of situations in which someone is absolutely right to the exclusion of any other point of view are small.

Chapter 11

Leadership

There have been a lot of books written on the topic of leadership. It is a hard thing to define exactly why some people inspire others to follow them. In a way, that ability is something that you cannot really teach to people—they either have it within them or they don't. In addition, leadership requirements differ depending on the area you are talking about. Political leadership differs from business leadership, which differs from moral or religious leadership, which differs from artistic leadership, which differs from military leadership. That said, however, there are a few aspects of leadership which are common to all areas and which can be learned.

Aristotle said that people need to be prudent. Notice that he did not just say that they had to be smart, because he knew that smart people can make major mistakes. **Prudence** is more than being smart. Prudence is being right about the future and taking actions that lead one on a good path into the future. Prudence is also about knowing how the world works and what human nature is like. In other words, it is a kind of practical wisdom. To be leader, you have to have the right overall strategy and make the right decisions. But these skills start with prudence. Another way of talking about prudence is simply to say that you have to have good judgment.

Another necessary, but not sufficient, quality of leadership is **competence**. No one is going to follow someone who doesn't know what he is doing or what he is talking about. Now, simply being competent doesn't make you a leader, but you rarely see good leaders that are also incompetent.

People want leaders to be strong. That means that a leader must be able to make tough decisions and stick to them. It also means that he must be able to take responsibility for the welfare of other people and not try to blame bad outcomes on things outside himself. A strong leader takes full personal responsibility for what is going on in his organization. It sometimes means that you come to the defense of people that work under you unless their behavior is unacceptable and cannot be defended. Strong leadership means having the courage to hold to a position because you think it is right, even though there is strong opposition to it. That means that playing politics is not always the same as good leadership.

Leadership is about relationships with other people and the ability to communicate ideas to them. Likability is a factor, too, because it is simply not easy to follow someone that you hate. That means that leadership is partly about integrity. People prefer someone who says what he means and means what he says and who holds himself to the same standard to which he holds other people. People don't like people who say one thing and do another. Integrity is also partly about credibility. People find it hard to follow someone that they think is lying to them. Morality is part of likability, but the fact is that there have been some strong leaders in history who were totally unethical.

To lead means almost by definition that you are willing to be out front of people a little bit, which means that you are willing to be out of sync with at least some people. But if you are totally out of sync with people, you run the risk that they won't follow you at all. If you are not willing to be bold and lead out front, then you're probably more of a manager than a leader.

So the bottom line is that leadership is about character, which is why, to some extent, it is innate in people. That said, people can learn to be better leaders, and the more leadership experience you have, the more likely you are to avoid making mistakes in your leadership style. When you operate in a leadership position, you always have to think about how the things you do and say make you look as a leader. When you make a decision or say something, it should be something that you can defend in public with a rational argument. If you can't defend it in public, then maybe it is not the kind of thing you should do or say.

A big part of practical leadership is the ability to judge character and ability in others. You need to hire people into key positions under you, and much of your success as a leader will depend on the success of the people you have working for you. That said, I'm not sure that the ability to judge people well can be taught in a textbook. Some people have the knack for seeing through people, and some just do not.

In a democracy, where power is decentralized and there are many special interests and competing factions, leadership is also partly about working with adversaries and people that just don't agree with you. If you don't have some ability to bring people together by finding common ground and using persuasion, it can be hard to lead a democracy. Of course, very few people get to lead a government. In most cases leaders are dealing with many different organizations outside their own, each with its own cultures and languages. Leadership in that context means being able to get people to work together in spite of the differences between organizations.

Chapter 12

Classical Music

Many people do not listen to classical music because they do not have direction on what to listen to. Classical music has survived the test of time, and there is a certain reliability that is associated with that survival. Listening to music without words forces you to derive meaning from the structure of the music, which is a higher level form of listening. I think most people can afford to have at least thirteen CDs of classical music in their collection, at a cost of about $250. So I'm going to recommend exactly thirteen classical compositions that can form the basis for a reasonable sampling of the classical tradition.

1: Bach, The Well Tempered Clavier, Book I. Bach wrote a prelude and fugue for each key that is available on the piano, and the results show a huge range of style and emotion. I think the Andras Schiff version is the best because he gets the most emotion out of the music, but a good faster recording was also done by Maurizio Pollini.

2: Beethoven, Symphonies nos. 5 and 7. Beethoven is a giant in music because of his towering imagination. His symphonies are big, architectural works that have a lot of drama. There are two performances of these symphonies that can be recommended, the Fritz Reiner/Chicago Symphony and the Carlos Kleiber/Vienna Philharmonic. The Reiner is more controlled and precise, and the Kleiber is more emotional and wild.

3: Brahms, Symphonies nos. 2 and 3. Brahms is one of the more emotional composers who writes directly from the heart. His symphonies are big and dramatic. A good pick is the Herbert von Karajan/Berlin Philharmonic recording or the George Szell/Cleveland Symphony version.

4: Chopin, Preludes. Chopin is one of the greatest composers for the piano. The preludes are a series of miniature compositions that show a wide range of structure and emotion. Chopin combines a Romantic approach with a very intellectual brain. I would recommend either the Maurizo Pollini performance or the one by Martha Argerich.

5: Mahler, Symphony no. 4. Mahler had deep emotions, but also a big brain. The Fourth Symphony is his softest and most pastoral, with a third movement that is from the heart. There are a lot of fine performances of this piece, but I would recommend getting either the Bernard Haitink/Royal Concertgebouw Orchestra performance with Christina Schafer as the soloist or the Klaus Tennstedt/London Philharmonic performance. There are actually a number of good performance of this piece. The Berlin Philharmonic plays it very well under either Bernard Haitink or Herbert von Karajan and the Cleveland Symphony plays it very well under either George Szell or Christoph von Dohnanyi. The Vienna Philharmonic performance under Lorin Maazel is also good.

6: Rimsky-Korsakov, *Scheherazade*. Rimsky-Korsakov had a good feel for orchestration, which is the process of choosing instruments to play various lines in the score. Scheherazade is a fantasy piece with a lot of beauty and color. I would get the Seiji Ozawa/Vienna Philharmonic or Boston Symphony Orchestra performance, or perhaps the older Leonard Bernstein/ New York Philharmonic reading.

7: Dvorak, Symphony no. 9, *From the New World*. Dvorak is a little corny, but he has a good understanding of what works musically for the audience. I would get either the Herbert von Karajan/ Berlin Philharmonic performance or the one by Fritz Reiner/ Chicago Symphony Orchestra.

8: Mozart, Piano Concertos nos. 19 and 23. All of Mozart's twenty-seven piano concertos are wonderful, particularly after about the first ten. The piano concerto suited Mozart's happy, stream-of-consciousness style of writing. I would get the Maurizio Pollini/Vienna Philharmonic performance of nos. 19 and 23. If one got ambitious and wanted to buy the entire set of twenty-seven piano concertos, then I can recommend the Murray Perahia/English Chamber Orchestra performance.

9: Berlioz, Symphony Fantastique. Symphony Fantastique comes earlier in the tradition, and for that reason shows incredible imagination and innovation. I would get either the Riccardo Muti/Philadelphia Orchestra performance or the older performance by Sir Thomas Beecham and the Orchestra National de la Radiodiffusion Francaise. The Beecham is a little heavy, but that's not a bad approach for this piece.

10: Tchaikovsky, *Swan Lake* and *Sleeping Beauty* excerpts. Tchaikovsky is a very melodic writer and has a good imagination. These ballet excerpts should be easy for almost anyone, even a child, to understand. I would get the Leopold Stokowski/Philharmonia Orchestra performance. I have not heard any performance of equal caliber.

11: Wagner, *The Ring of the Nibelungs* excerpts. Wagner is a little misunderstood because people associate him with Nazism. Actually, Wagner came before the Nazis, and it wasn't really his fault that they adopted him. He was an anti-Semite, however. The Ring of the Nibelungs is actually a four-opera saga, but these excerpts capture the most exciting parts of the music.

I would get the Georg Solti/Vienna Philharmonic performance because the selection is right on.

12: Ravel, *Daphnis et Chloe* Suite no. 2. This is a work of fantasy
imagination. The Suite no. 2 is the last third or so of a larger
complete ballet, so you have to be careful in buying CDs. The
complete ballet is probably too hard and too long for most
people to appreciate, so I recommend just the Suite no. 2. I
can recommend either the Leonard Bernstein/New York
Philharmonic performance or the Leonard Slatkin/St. Louis
Symphony performance.

13: Johann Strauss, Waltzes. Johann Strauss captures a turn-
of-the-nineteeth-century, aristocratic, joy-of-life sentiment
that is unique in music. I would get either the Herbert von
Karajan/Berlin Philharmonic or the Wili Boskovsky/Vienna
Philharmonic.

Now that's not everything, and it leaves out some important
composers, but it is a credible core collection that for most people will probably completely satisfy their need to listen to classical
music. Of course, if one develops an interest, one can go further
and buy beyond these thirteen CDs.

Chapter 13

Literature

One of the reasons to read literature is to get a feel for the culture that produced it. Like all art, literature is a product of the moment in history from which it comes, and it reflects the world around it. Peering into that world can be a useful addition to reading straight expository history. I will offer a list of ten works of literature that both entertain and provide insight into cultural history.

1: William Shakespeare, *Hamlet, the Prince of Denmark.* Arguably Shakespeare's greatest play, *Hamlet* is about a great man whose destiny was thwarted and turned toward revenge and tragedy.
2: Thomas Hardy, *Tess of the d'Urbervilles.* A peek into British emotionalism, with the smatterings of philosophy that mark Thomas Hardy's style.
3: H. G. Wells, *Tono-Bungay.* A tale on the lighter side about capitalism, but hits hard on the class warfare that marks British culture.
4: E. M. Forster, *A Passage to India.* A look at British colonialism and its clash-of-culture consequences.

5: F. Scott Fitzgerald, *The Great Gatsby.* A nice look into a period in American history in which the American character was fully developed, but still harboring strong class-based thinking which was a holdover from European culture, mainly Britain.

6: Ernest Hemingway, *The Old Man and the Sea.* A simple story written in a very simple way which embodies the American style.

7: Stephen King, *The Shining.* A look into the American horror genre, notable because of the deep psychological analysis of the three main characters, who are father, mother, and son.

8: Johann Wolfgang von Goethe, *The Sorrows of Young Werther.* A tragic story of young love that gives a good insight into the emotional angst and turmoil that can exist under the seemingly cool German exterior.

9: Fyodor Dostoevsky, *Crime and Punishment.* A taste of Russian introspection on the dark side of humanity.

10: Peter Hoeg, *Smilla's Sense of Snow.* A taste of Danish literature, notable because of the coherence of the overall artistic vision and its treatment of a clash of cultures.

Chapter 14

Political Philosophy

Philosophy is largely a dead area of inquiry, but there are five works of political philosophy that explore the way we govern our societies and are useful to know.

1: Plato, *The Republic*. Plato takes us through a series of stories that teach us about the principles of governing a society.
2: St. Augustine, *The City of God*. St. Augustine formulates how a worldly society should be constructed in accordance with Christian ideas.
3: Thomas Hobbes, *Leviathan*. Hobbes justifies his theory that a strong government is needed to run a society.
4: Jean-Jacques Rousseau, *The Social Contract*. Rousseau lays a foundation for the idea that a government must be run with the consent of the governed.
5: John Locke, *Two Treatises of Civil Government*. Locke formulates some of the key ideas which formed the foundation for the creation of the United States, including the idea that we have the right to pursue life, liberty, and property.

These works are difficult to read because the language is from an earlier period of history, but they will give you a sense of how the history of political ideas developed over time in Europe. You should also note that I left out Karl Marx. Although he is important historically, his political philosophy has been largely discredited by trial and error (and a trail of dead bodies). In fact, I left out many books of political philosophy simply because if you are given too long a list, the costs of the time spent reading will outweigh the benefits.

Chapter 15

U.S. History Basics

Every American citizen should know the basic outline of U.S. history.

The first successful settlement of colonialists in America was a colony of British merchants in Jamestown, Virginia, in 1606. In 1620, the Pilgrims, a group of religious dissenters from Britain, arrived first at Cape Cod Bay, Massachusetts, and later relocated to Plymouth in Massachusetts. Other colonists followed, mostly from Britain but also from the Netherlands. At first it was a life-and-death struggle to survive, but by 1730 there were around 629,000 English settlers, and, by 1770, 2,148,000 settlers. Thus, there was a huge growth in population in the American colonies in the first 150 years. The North was heavily reliant on trade, while the South was heavily reliant on cash crops.

British law governed trade and taxation in the American colonies. Among the main laws were the Navigation Acts, passed between 1651 and 1696, which attempted to monopolize the profits of the carrying trade. Enforcement of these laws was lax until after 1763. In addition, heavy taxes were imposed by Britain in the form of the Sugar Act of 1764 and the Stamp Act of 1765. These attacks on profits in the colonies provoked a reaction, including invention of the slogan "no taxation without representation." The colonists had been relatively independent businessmen for a long time, and the crackdown by Britain struck not only at the pocketbook, but at the notions of freedom that the colonists held. From 1766 to 1775, discontent with British control of the colonies grew, and in 1775 the American Revolution broke out. In 1776, Thomas Jefferson wrote the Declaration of Independence, which declared the independence of the American colonies from Britain. It was a difficult war for the colonists, and at times they seemed on the verge of defeat. The Revolutionary War ended in 1781, when the revolutionary army commanded by George Washington defeated the British at Yorktown. The Articles of Confederation were ratified in 1781. The U.S. Constitution was signed on September 17, 1787, establishing a federal government with limited powers, with all other powers delegated to the several States. George Washington became the first president of the United States in 1789.

In the early days of the United States, there was a debate between Thomas Jefferson, who served as president, and Alexander Hamilton, who served as secretary of the treasury. Jefferson favored a small federal government and an agrarian economy. Hamilton favored a strong federal government and emphasized finance and manufacturing. Over time this debate was played out as America moved towards industrialization and Hamilton won the argument. America was pushing westward, occupying new lands and making them into new states. The process took a century to complete but was entirely effective, much to the dismay of the indigenous Indian population and the European countries that tried to lay claims to parts of the American continent. Americans dug canals, built roads, and constructed railroads, as cities sprang up across the country. President James Monroe (1758–1831) established the Monroe Doctrine, which held that "the American continents, by the free and independent condition which they have assumed and maintain, are henceforth not to be considered as subjects for future colonization by any European powers."

The United States was much richer in 1860 than it had been in 1800. Population had increased from five million to thirty-one million and was growing at a rate of about 35 percent per decade. In 1845, a journalist declared that it was America's "manifest destiny to overspread the continent allotted by Providence for the free development of our yearly multiplying millions." Government policy supported this idea. The Homestead Act of 1862 gave 160 acres of free western land to anyone willing to settle on it for at least five years.

Slavery of blacks had been a feature of American society since the early days of colonization, but increasingly over time and starting officially in 1831, there was a rift between those in the North who favored abolition of slavery, largely on religious grounds, and those in the South who viewed it as a necessary part of their agrarian economy. The debate carried into presidential politics, but Abraham Lincoln beat out the Southern Democratic candidate for the presidency. Shortly thereafter, southern states began to secede from the United States and formed themselves into the Confederacy. President Lincoln conducted a war against the Confederacy from 1861 to 1865, a bloody civil war that claimed many American lives. The Confederate Army was led by Robert E. Lee and the Union Army ultimately by Ulysses S. Grant. President Lincoln issued the Emancipation Proclamation to free slaves. In the end, the Union prevailed and the Confederacy was defeated. On April 14, 1865, President Lincoln was shot in the head by a Southern sympathizer named John Wilkes Booth, and died a day later. A thirteenth amendment was added to the U.S. Constitution that declared slavery unconstitutional. The years following the Civil War, known as Reconstruction, were difficult because of the damage that had been done both physically and also psychologically by the war. The Ku Klux Klan began during this period as a white supremacist group dedicated to the oppression and disenfranchisement of blacks. Many Southern states passed laws disenfranchising blacks by making it harder for them to vote There were numerous lynchings of blacks by whites.

The Industrial Revolution continued the transformation of American society with steamboats, telegraph, and railroads, all bringing producers and consumers closer together in integrated markets. Some men became powerful in business, such as Andrew Carnegie, the steel magnate; J. P. Morgan, the banker; and John D. Rockefeller, the oil baron. The period from the end of the Civil War to 1929 was a period of robust capitalism, with rapid expansion in the American economy. Indeed, the power of big business in America became such that President Theodore Roosevelt advocated for a big government that could oppose the power of big business. This era saw the creation of antitrust laws to discourage monopolistic behavior on the part of business. This era also saw the creation of the Federal Reserve in 1913 as a central bank that would be the banker of last resort and which could manipulate the currency, hopefully to help avoid the kinds of financial crises which the business cycle had produced. The rise of big business was followed the rise of big labor unions to act as a counterweight to the power of management.

Woodrow Wilson was elected president in 1912, and he led the nation through the First World War, which was primarily a European dispute. In the end, America and its allies won the First World War. Under Woodrow Wilson's guidance, a League of Nations was established. Unfortunately, the Treaty of Versailles that set the peace imposed such punitive sanctions on Germany that another war was almost inevitable.

In 1920, the Nineteenth Amendment to the Constitution was passed, giving women the right to vote. In the 1920s America enjoyed enormous prosperity, particularly in its stock market, but in 1929 the stock market crashed and America was propelled into a severe depression. The depression was made worse due to some governmental actions, such as the enactment of the Smoot-Hawley tariff in 1930. The years 1933 and 1934 saw the creation of Depression-era legislation to correct for the financial excesses of the 1920s, including the creation of the securities laws and the Glass-Steagall Act, which separated the functions of banks, insurance companies, and securities firms. In 1930, the Food and Drug Administration was created. In 1933, Franklin Roosevelt became president of the United States. He attempted various governmental interventions, called the New Deal, designed to spur the economy through spending and governmental job creation following the economic theories of John Maynard Keynes. Historians dispute the effectiveness of these interventions, and some believe they actually made the economy worse. Part of the New Deal that survives today is the Social Security Act of 1935, which promised income support to the elderly. The year 1935 also saw the passage of the National Labor Relations Act, which guarantees the right of U.S. workers to form unions and engage in collective bargaining.

On December 7, 1941, the Japanese launched an air attack on the Pearl Harbor naval installation, severely damaging the U.S. fleet. Shortly thereafter, Adolf Hitler declared war against the United States. This had the effect of drawing America into the Second World War with the Axis powers, namely the imperialist Japanese, Italian Fascists, and Nazi Germany. The war effort was immense, with unprecedented government spending, and it had the effect of bringing the United States out of the Depression. Adolf Hitler had embarked upon a belligerent war policy towards his neighbors and a homicidal policy towards certain citizen minorities, most notably Jews. President Franklin Roosevelt led the country during this promethean battle. It took four years of all-out fighting alongside our historical ally Britain, with the loss of millions of lives, but in the end Germany and Japan were defeated in 1945. It is worth noting that Russia fought with the Allies against the Axis powers during this conflict.

The victory of World War II left the United States in a favorable position with respect to the rest of the world. America was both the supreme military power and the manufacturing leader because, to put it colloquially, Europe was in rubble and Asia was a rice paddy. The Great Depression was largely ended by the robust economic activity of World War II. Following the war, America led an effort to help rebuild Europe and Japan economically so that they could eventually become free and peaceful nations. In the end, Germany and Japan would become strong allies of the United States. The 1950s and 1960s were a period of prosperity for America and saw the construction of a federal highway system under President Dwight D. Eisenhower, who had also served in World War II as the supreme Allied commander.

The nuclear era began with the bombing by the United States of the Japanese cities of Hiroshima and Nagasaki with nuclear bombs, something President Harry S. Truman had felt was necessary to end the war quickly without further bloodshed. Following the end of World War II, a Cold War began between the United States as the leading democratic powers and the Soviet Union and China as the leading communist powers. During this period, the threat of nuclear war hung over the heads of the world's population. At home, an unscrupulous senator named Joseph McCarthy conducted a witch hunt against suspected communists in America which destroyed numerous lives. The nuclear tension between the Soviet Union and the United States reached a peak in the Cuban Missile Crisis in 1962, in which the Soviets constructed a missile launch pad in Cuba and President John F. Kennedy dispatched the U.S. Navy to blockade Cuba to get the Soviets to stand down.

The United States fought two wars as part of its policy to contain communism: the Korean War in the 1950s and the Vietnam War in the 1960s to early 1970s. In the Korean War, the United States was able to repel the North Korean invasion back to a midpoint on the Korean peninsula. In the Vietnam War, the United States withdrew after suffering fifty thousand casualties and a potent antiwar protest at home, and South Vietnam ultimately fell to the North Vietnamese communists. The United States also fought a proxy war when the Soviet Union invaded and occupied Afghanistan in the 1980s and we supported the Afghan insurgents. After a nine-year battle, the Soviet Union was forced to leave Afghanistan.

At home in the United States, there was unrest over discrimination against blacks. In 1954, the U.S. Supreme Court ruled in *Brown v. Board of Education of Topeka* that segregated schools were an unconstitutional violation of equal protection under the Fourteenth Amendment. In the early 1960s, black leaders such as the Reverend Dr. Martin Luther King led protests against race discrimination. This cause was taken up first by President John F. Kennedy and later by President Lyndon Johnson. President Kennedy was assassinated in November 1963. In 1964 and 1965, civil rights laws were enacted to make race and gender discrimination illegal, and the Voting Rights Act was enacted to protect the voting rights of blacks. President Johnson also presided over the "Great Society" reforms in Congress in 1965 that created Medicare, the health insurance program for the elderly, and Medicaid, the health insurance program for the poor. In 1969, America landed the first manned mission on the moon, just eight years after President Kennedy had called for it in his inaugural address.

President Richard Nixon ended the Vietnam War and began a diplomatic relationship with China that continues to this day, but was forced to resign from his second term because he had covered up illegal acts that were done during his re-election campaign in a scandal known as Watergate. Nixon's successor, Gerald Ford, pardoned Nixon for his actions taken while president because Ford thought it was best for the country to move forward.

President Jimmy Carter was plagued by a bad economy with high inflation, high interest rates, and stagnant growth, a phenomenon called "stagflation." Towards the end of his presidency, the Iranian revolutionary government took over the American embassy in Tehran and held American diplomats hostage. President Carter's inability to resolve the situation and his poor performance on the economy ensured that he would be a one-term president, despite such achievements as brokering a peace between Israel and Egypt.

President Ronald Reagan was elected in 1980 and promised a conservative approach with a smaller government, lower taxes, and less regulation. He achieved the last two goals, but failed to achieve significant spending cuts. The government continued to grow and deficits were used to compensate for a lower tax policy. President Reagan had a strong belief in the power of capitalism, and he waged a stiff defense spending battle against the Soviet Union. Going against the advice of his own State Department, he called the Soviet Union the "evil empire." He found a partner in a Soviet premier named Mikhail Gorbachev, who knew the days of the Soviet Union were numbered because its economic system and oppressive government were not sustainable. Although many factors resulted in the fall of the Soviet Union and the end of the cold war, President Reagan can lay claim to having played at least some role in the outcome. President Reagan's support for the monetary policies of Federal Reserve Board Chairman Paul Volcker helped end the stagflation of the 1970s and, together with the improvements in tax policy and regulatory policy, he set the stage for the economic recovery of the 1990s.

It should be noted that since FDR, the federal government has generally pursued Keynesian economic policy that advocates economic stimulus through tax cuts or government spending increases. Since Woodrow Wilson, the federal government has steadily increased its power by enacting federal laws and programs, including the entitlement programs known as Social Security, Medicare, and Medicaid. As a result of these policies, the United States has ended up in the early twenty-first century with a mountain of debt and unfunded liabilities.

The basic facts stop at this point under the general premise that it takes some time for the view of history to become clear.

Bibliography for Chapter 15

Atack, J., and P. Passell. *A New Economic View of American History from Colonial Times to 1940* (W. W. Norton & Company, 1994).

Brogan, H. *The Penguin History of the United States* (Penguin Books, 1985).

Heilbroner, R., and A. Singer. *The Economic Transformation of America: 1600 to the Present* (Harcourt Brace College Publishers, 1994).

Johnson, P. *A History of the American People* (HarperCollins Publishers, 1997).

Menzin, M., C. Podraza, and S. Alexander. *The Beford Glossary for U.S. History* (Bedford/St. Martin's, 2007).

Chapter 16

Health Care Costs

Rising health care costs are a major problem. If we don't get a handle on that, the health care financing system is going to buckle, and there may be future compromises in both the access to, and quality of, health care.

The first point to make is that health insurers are financing entities. In other words, they are pass-throughs. Some people think of an insurer as if it were a bank account where you put money in over time and it builds up and then, at some point in the future, you withdraw the money. Not so. Each year, the insurer will collect money to cover its claims, plus administrative expenses, plus a return. Money flows in the front door and right out the back door.

The big problem is rising health care costs. That is most of what is driving premiums higher. The health care system and health care financing system are inherently inflationary.

One reason for increasing costs is simply that medical science is better than it used to be. Back in Mozart's day, going to the doctor might have meant getting a nice bloodletting or having a leech applied to your body. If you had to have surgery, there was no anesthetic and no antiseptic. If you managed not to die soon after due to infection or shock, you were lucky. Under these conditions, of course health care costs were lower than they are today. We can do a lot more for people today than we used to be able to do. If we look forward into the future, should we not expect medical science to continue to progress and costs to go up? Maybe medicine becomes more cost efficient, or maybe it just keeps getting more expensive. At some point, perhaps medical care will be like what we see in *Star Trek* and will be low cost, but that is probably a long ways off.

Another reason for increasing costs is that we are victims of our own success. People live a lot longer than they did in Mozart's day, which is probably due to a variety of factors, but no doubt it is partly attributable to better medical care. One of the benefits (to others) of dying young, as Mozart did at thirty-five, is that you are no longer a drain on the health care system. The longer you live, presumably the more you cost. Some people say that 70 percent of health care costs are for the treatment of chronic diseases. But some of these diseases are old-age diseases. And of course, end-of-life care can also get expensive. I'm not advocating that you shoot yourself in the head tonight to save money on health care costs, but you see the point I am making. You should also note that 80 percent of the gains in longevity over the past 150 years are due to public health efforts, such as sanitation and vaccination, not medical care.

Another issue is our method of compensation. Generally, most health insurers pay doctors on a per-procedure basis. The more procedures you do, the more money you make. That is obviously an inflationary incentive. When you couple it with the doctor's desire to do all that he can for his patients and the desire not to get sued for malpractice, we shouldn't be that surprised that costs tend to go up.[6] Now there are some other compensation mod-

---

6   Another aspect of the medical malpractice issue beyond defensive medicine is the need to buy state-of-the-art equipment. Of course, state-of-the-art equipment is also about marketing and competition.

els out there. Kaiser Permanente[7] pays doctors a fixed salary, as does a single-payer system like Britain's. Does this reduce costs? You would expect it to, but I haven't gotten hold of any hard data on that. Some people are proposing compensating doctors not for each procedure, but for an episode of care, but this is just an idea at this stage. Of course, some insurers are testing out incentives for quality care and good outcomes, but I haven't seen solid data on the cost effectiveness of this approach.

Finally, let me interject some harsh reality. One man's costs are another man's revenues. So we can keep hitting on top of the idea of adjusting provider reimbursements, but is it realistic to think that we are going to get there? If it takes seventeen years to implement a new standard of care, as reported by the American Medical Association, how fast can we move in any event? There has been some movement towards pay-for-performance schemes in medicine that focus on outcomes instead of volume of procedures, but the jury is still out on how effective this will be at reducing costs.

Let's talk about consumer-driven health care. Some thinkers made a big deal out of this in trying to market high-deductible policies with a medical or health savings account. Now, I support high-deductible policies. But I for one tend to do what the doctor tells me to do. If he orders me to take medicine or to have a procedure done, I do it. If I get cancer, did I choose to get cancer? In other words, I am not the consumer in the sense of making free choices. The doctor is driving the consumption, and we already talked about the incentives that he has. It is not the same thing as the market for cheeseburgers, where if the price goes up you just choose to stop buying. Health care consumption is what the economists call **price inelastic**, particularly as the health condition gets more serious and life threatening. If you need to buy something, then the price tends to go up.

Some of our health issues are probably driven by demographics (like the baby boomers), lifestyle (food we eat, smoking, lack of exercise, drinking), toxins in the food and in the environment.

---

7   The Mayo Clinic in Rochester, Minnesota, does the same.

In addition, we know that health is related to socioeconomic factors such as education and wealth. Health is a complex thing, but the point is that most costs are related to things outside the health care delivery system.

Let's talk about the role of insurance in costs. Now obviously, insurance is the best thing that ever happened to the health care industry because it enables it to do more at higher cost. But we can't really get rid of it, because medical costs are so high that very few people can handle them. I totally support insurance for health care finance. But, let's focus a moment on some of the incentives. If a patient is insulated from the costs of health care, then he doesn't have much incentive to control costs or to live a healthy lifestyle. Of course, there are usually cost-sharing provisions in a health plan, which can help create some good incentives. However, you should note that there is some debate on this issue. Does cost-sharing reduce unnecessary utilization, or does it deter people from seeking needed care that might help avoid even more serious costs down the road? I'm not sure we have clear data on that point.

Finally, there is the issue of the supply of doctors and nurses. There are a few people that think that the more doctors you have, the more procedures they do, and the higher the costs. However, the standard economics analysis is that if the supply is inadequate and the demand goes up, prices tend to be higher. However, whatever view one takes, the point is that there is a relationship between the number of providers our schools are churning out and health care costs. Note that hospitals and other large care facilities are a different matter. There are regulatory requirements that result in a minimum level of fixed costs. Because of that, competition can actually be a problem, because if certain pieces of a hospital's business get stripped away, the entire hospital can become unable to meet it basic fixed costs. In other words, normal supply and demand don't work the same in the health care delivery area. Then get rid of regulation? For example, do we really want to remove minimum standards in hospitals for the ratio of doctors and nurses to patients? Maybe that's not such a good idea. Also note that when there is a high barrier to entry to supply, such as with doctors or drugs, the price tends to be higher.

Democrats believe that state health insurance exchanges will lower health care costs through competition. Republicans believe that selling health insurance across state lines will lower health care costs through competition. Both are wrong. The market for health insurance is a separate and distinct market from the market for health care. It is in the health care market that costs are rising, forcing premiums to go up. As any businessperson knows, while competition may reduce prices, it cannot reduce the underlying costs that went into running the business, because the costs arise in different markets.

What are the solutions? Actually, the more you know, the more skeptical you become that there are any really effective solutions to health care cost control. I don't intend to spend a lot of time on the various ideas that are floating around out there, because you can look into them yourself. However, it pays to think critically about it, because some people are selling Kool-Aid on this topic. We have a serious problem and we need serious solutions, and pretending something is a solution when it is not is not productive.

If there is a solution to the cost problem, it probably has a lot to do with changing behavior. Nutrition, exercise, smoking, drinking: these are the issues. Is changing behavior easy? No, but it has to be a focus. Incentives may be needed.

Another tactic that might help is trying to push some care from doctors to nurses and other care practitioners so that people are practicing at the top of their licenses and we have a lower-cost alternative to physician-delivered care.

Finally, some people advocate increased attention to care as a way of lowering costs. The idea is that if people get the right kind of care, more serious problems can be avoided later. But this is still in the early stages of development.

Let me end with just an observation from my work in this area. When people are healthy, all they care about is premium costs. But when they get really sick, particularly when their lives are at stake, all they think about is coverage, and money is no object. Similarly, it may seem tempting to squash down on the doctors' compensation to lower costs, but if it lowers the quality of health care, then you get hurt. So you have to kind of see it from both sides, because you actually are on both sides.

Chapter 17

Rhetoric

Rhetoric is the art of using words and arguments to make a point.

When arguing, the most important thing is to be brief. You should get to the point as quickly as possible. When writing, the rule to remember is Strunk and White's rule number 4 to "eliminate unnecessary words."

Lying or exaggerating is generally not a good approach in trying to win an argument, because it tends to destroy your credibility. One way of enhancing your credibility is to make sure that your statements read as fact instead of opinion. For example, if I say, "Global warming is caused by man," that is an opinion that could be disputed. But if I say, "A majority of scientists believe that global warming is partially caused by man," then that is closer to a fact. If you deal in facts, you will have credibility. If you just deal in your own opinions, people can easily disregard you.

Lawyers argue only one side of the issue because that is the way the legal system is set up. But, generally, it can be somewhat ineffective to argue only one side of the question, because it again affects your credibility. If you are not able to deal with all the key issues that are in play, it makes it look as if you are unable to engage the opposing side on some points, or even that you don't understand some aspects of the situation. It is better to try to deal with all the key issues and not leave anything out, even if the issue is not 100 percent favorable to your side.

Whatever you do, make sure your argument makes sense. Senator John Kerry ran for president under the theory that his being a Vietnam veteran meant that he should be the president. That theory doesn't even make logical sense. His opponent, George W. Bush, had a better argument—that "you don't change quarterbacks in the middle of a football game," where the wars in Iraq and Afghanistan were the analogy to the football game. That argument actually does make sense, even if the rhetoric is dumbed all the way down. If you want an argument to resonate with people, it has to make sense.

When writing a letter, it is a good idea to shoot for one to two pages, because it is doubtful many people will carefully read anything longer. I have gone as long as eight pages in writing a letter, but that was only because I was doing a full exposition of a rather complicated issue and was actually trying to show people how complex things were to deter them from acting. Normally I write a very short letter under the assumption that people simply do not have the time for anything else. Writing a short letter means that you have to get your thoughts together about what you are trying to say. When I write a letter, I try to take all the emotions out of it so that the letter reads like pure reason. But that is more of a personal style point than an absolute rule.

When doing an oral presentation, the key is to have good organization. PowerPoint helps in this regard by forcing you to address topics that fit in small slides. If you do not have a good organization, it may be difficult for the audience to follow what you are saying. Also, when I do oral arguments, I usually try to make one to three points stand out to the listener. The reason is that people will tend to forget what you say, so you have to organize your speech around some basic points and hit those points hard, perhaps even with some repetition. Also, you need to observe the general rule about getting to the point quickly; otherwise, people may not be able to follow you.

Using examples or cases can be an effective way to illustrate a point, but the story needs to be short enough that it can hold people's attention. Examples are also an opportunity to bring emotion into the arena. For many years in human history, people told parables or stories or allegories to illustrate deeper thoughts, and these are still good ways of making an argument.

Identifying the issues and then providing an answer to each issue can be an effective way to organize a speech or a piece of writing.

An effective way to attack an argument is to illustrate the absurdity of it. Normally the form of that attack is something like "if that is true, then it must mean that X."

You have to be careful with analogies, because no two things are really the same unless they are the same thing. If you drill down into the details of analogies, they often begin to fall apart.

Personal, or **ad hominem**, attacks should be avoided. Any debate should be on the merits of the issues, not on the merits of the messenger. If you think you need to discredit your opponent, the best way to do it is to repeat that he said or did something wrong or foolish, as an illustration of how dumb or crazy he is. That way you are dealing in fact and not stating a personal opinion about character. In other words, state facts and let others draw their own conclusions. It is generally a bad idea to make accusations against someone because accusations are often hard to prove. It is particularly difficult to prove that someone is acting in bad faith or from improper motives.

If you are arguing a public policy issue, the most effective line of attack is to show the ways in which the policy won't work or will create bad consequences. Arguing philosophy with politicians is generally less effective than arguing pragmatism. What a politician is worrying about is how a policy can come back to bite him later.

Finally, there is the issue of consistency of rhetoric. The reality is that no conversation is private, in the sense that the things you say to someone can be repeated to other people. As a result, it is better not to say things to anyone that you couldn't get behind publicly if they were reported in the newspaper. Another way to say this is that it is better not to be two-faced when talking to people. But the idea is to have consistent rhetoric to enhance your credibility. If you don't say incendiary things in public, then you shouldn't say them in private, either, because there is no such thing as a truly private conversation. In the old days, before there were video cameras everywhere and a twenty-four-hour cable news cycle, you might get away with a little inconsistency here and there, but not with modern communications.

Chapter 18

Military Policy

To win a war requires troops, weapons, and sustained funding. A national commitment is required, and that means political support and the support of the public. For this reason, no war should be undertaken unless it is clearly necessary. A necessary war should be relatively easy to justify to the public and gain support. If a war is not necessary, then you might not find the national commitment that is necessary to win it. For this reason alone, fighting a war just because it seems like a good idea to do it is generally a bad idea. Another way to think of it is simply to say that it is immoral to put American soldiers in harm's way unless it is a necessity.

The question is what constitutes a necessity. Clearly, if we are attacked, then we need to respond in order to send a message that attacking the United States is a bad idea. Beyond that, to justify any war, there must be a grave national security interest at stake, and the danger to Americans should be clear and present. When we get into more remote justifications for war that are about protecting the American way of life, such as wars over resources or wars over economic issues, we need to think carefully about it.

Under the Constitution, the Congress must declare war. This is a good procedural check to make sure that the war is necessary and has sufficient support to be successful, but in fact we have not always strictly followed the rule. One of the good things about making sure that a war is a necessary war is that it tends to solve the problem of having clear objectives and a defined exist strategy, both of which are important for the military to understand in carrying out its mission.

The best way to win a battle is through overwhelming force. Of course, that is not always possible, but that is the ideal situation. Rarely is air and sea power alone enough to win a battle. Normally, to achieve military objectives, it requires ground troops and a lot of them. People that say that you can do better with a smaller footprint are ignoring the history of warfare.

Weakness in military preparedness can invite attack. The purpose of a strong military is to create deterrence that will stop others from acting badly before they do so. The stronger you are, the less likely it will be that you have to pull the trigger. If people always behaved nicely then we wouldn't need defense spending to act as a deterrent, but if history is any guide, it tells us that weakness invites aggression. Financial capability to fund an extended war is a big part of military preparedness.

We don't know all of the circumstances under which our military will be called upon to act in the future, so above all things we must have a military with flexibility and a range of capabilities. Having that sort of military takes a lot of money.

If you're outgunned or outmanned, then you should avoid the conflict.

It is a good idea to recognize that war can lead to a lot of unintended consequences because of its inherent unpredictability. The other problem with war is that in order to make your opponent pay a price, you also have to pay a price. So you need to take the measure of your opponent and determine his will and ability to pay the price as compared to your own.

Finally, military objectives are often not the whole story. Often there is a political or diplomatic objective that goes beyond achievement of the military objective. If the military objective is not the whole story, then military policy cannot be the whole solution. A word might be said about the regime-change policy that we have used the military to implement in the recent past. In foreign policy we are talking about government-to-government relations, and whether we agree with everything the government does entirely is not the issue. We take governments as we find them and, given that many of them have legitimate claim to exercise sovereign power, we ought to be somewhat humble about trying to change them into something they are not. In this regard, diplomacy for the purpose of suggesting changes is a lot different than forcing change at gunpoint. There are practical limits to military power and our foreign policy needs to be adjusted to recognize those practical limits.

Chapter 19

Going into the Workplace

Going into the workplace requires some caution because it can be a minefield if you don't operate smoothly.

Workplaces can be gossip mills, so generally you don't want to talk about your private life in the workplace. You want to have a public face, in much the same way that a politician does, that you present at work. You want people to see your professional side, and you don't want them to have too much detail beyond that. If you are going to say something in the office to someone, it needs to be the kind of thing that you can get behind publicly, because what you say can be repeated to others and sometimes lose something in the translation.

It is important to be polite in the workplace. That means saying things like "please" and "thank you." Part of this means respecting the hierarchy, so when you talk to people who are of higher rank, you should call them Mr. ____ or Ms. ____ unless they have given you permission to use their first names. In addition, when you are in a meeting and someone asks a question, you shouldn't answer if someone more senior is supposed to answer. Don't be late to a meeting. Important people might be able to make others wait for them, but when you're just starting out, you cannot do that. Arrive early and have chats with people who also arrive early. It's a good way of finding out things.

Normally, you should use writing for setting down the record. Although some things are confidential, many things can be obtained through litigation discovery. What you want the written record to reflect is professional, official action and deliberation. You have to think about how a jury might view what you are writing. In particular, e-mail can be a problem because people sometimes use it as a substitute for conversation when it should definitely not be used for that purpose. If you want to have a conversation off the record, then pick up the telephone or walk into someone's office and have a face-to-face conversation. Don't put it in writing in an e-mail that a lawyer can get hold of it. In particular, if you are putting something on company letterhead, it needs to be the kind of statement that can hold up as an official public communication. When you start out, it may be the case that any communications you write that are directed outside the office should go to your boss first for a quick review. Check with your boss to see if this is how he wants to handle things. It may seem like micromanagement, but it is a good way of decreasing the error rate. As you increase in proficiency, you may be delegated more latitude.

If you have questions, ask your boss. It is a sign of intelligence to ask questions. Don't just go out and start doing things the wrong way. You should respect the chain of command, which means that communications up and down the hierarchy should follow that hierarchy. This means that you don't communicate to your boss's superior directly about something that should go through your boss to the superior. It also means that you should be careful to make sure that when you do something, you have the authority to do it. You don't want to be making decisions or giving orders about things that are really your boss's prerogative to handle. In this regard, it is a good idea to find out early on who is in charge of what in the organization. If there are procedures set forth for doing things, you should follow them, because procedures are designed to reduce the error rate, often by imposing checks and balances.

If the office has a dress code, you should follow it, because you always want to look professional. Overdressing can be a problem in some places as well. For example, if your boss wears a blue shirt, you might not want to wear a white shirt. Or if your boss wears a navy blue suit, you might want to avoid wearing a suit with pinstripes. In general, you can take your dressing cues from management.

Insubordination can get you fired. Insubordination occurs when you don't follow orders or you are giving your boss unnecessary blowback in the ordinary course of doing work. Now, you probably should not follow an illegal order, and it can sometimes be helpful to talk about the best course of action, but, in general, once something has been decided it is best to accept it and move on with your life.

One trick to keeping the workflow moving is to sort your tasks into things that can be done quickly and things that take a long time to do. If you do the things that can be done quickly right away all the time, then you will tend to be an efficient worker. It is generally a mistake to just pile things up in the order in which they came in and handle them in the same order. You have to be strategic about what you work on first.

If you get to be a manager, remember that your job is not to do everything yourself, but to get others to do things for you. I like to delegate quite a bit because it increases the worker's sense of personal responsibility. I don't like to give orders, because I prefer that people give themselves orders. It is better for them psychologically, and easier for me because I don't have to keep after them every five seconds. Of course, you can't delegate so much that you lose sight of what is going on around you. If you give an order, make sure it is crystal clear. Operating under confusing orders can be very frustrating for subordinates. If you have to criticize someone, do it in private. If you're running a meeting, start on time and be quick about handling the meeting. People have a lot of other things to do besides sit in a meeting that meanders all over the place.

Before going into a workplace, it might make sense to read a book on interpersonal relations and how to handle them. A classic in this area is Dale Carnegie's *How to Win Friends and Influence People* (1936). In the end, the business environment is all about relationships. Also, you should be aware that every organization has its own culture, and it is a good idea to try to fit into that culture while you are there. One indispensible rule is to try to always be a good listener. If you listen to what people are saying and you know what is going on around you, you should do okay.

I will note one minor point which is really just a personal pet peeve. When leaving voice messages, start with your name, and say your telephone number twice. Then just leave a brief message. Don't try to have an entire conversation on a voice mail recording. The reason I say that is that it takes a lot of time to go through phone messages, and one thing you don't want to have to do is listen to a phone message twice, particularly a long one. If the person you're calling can pick up your name and phone number right away, that is really all he needs to get back to you.

When you go into the workplace, you should be aware that one day you may leave the workplace and try to find another job. If you do that, your future employers may call your past employers to find out about you. Normally, when you look for a job you need references. When I am calling references, I normally ask how the person did in his job, but also how well he got along with other people, and whether he was able to work both independently and also as a team player. After many years of working with people, you find out that it is not just about what people know, but what their behavior is like.

Bottom line, surviving in a workplace means doing your job well and making sure your communications send the right message about you. Part of getting along with people in the workplace means understanding that every organization has its own culture, language, and norms.

Chapter 20

The Problem with Running the Government like a Business

Every now and then a businessman runs for political office and claims that he wants to run government like a business. It sounds good. But there are many ways in which government is not at all like a business, and in fact we would not want it to be.

Government is not supposed to make a profit. We fund government through our taxes and debt, and we don't want to pay a profit margin on top of that. But more importantly, you can only make a profit where people are both willing and able to pay money, and that focus is very different from a tax-funded government because government is able to help people regardless of how much money they have. In that regard, government has a fundamentally different purpose from business.

There is a downside to the idealistic focus of government. Without a profit motive, you have to have another basis for deciding what to do. Both businesses and government serve the public, but the government serves the public without really asking the public very carefully whether it should be doing what it is doing. A business knows it is serving the public because it gets paid directly for the services. If a business is no longer useful, it simply goes away. A government program exists because a legislature has ordained it, but whether it is really effective at serving the public is harder to know because there is no profit margin to judge it by. Profit is the yardstick by which business is judged. But what is the yardstick for government? Other than a general sense that government should be in the public interest, no one has developed a clear yardstick for government. Sometimes government programs stay around longer than they should.

Because government does not have a profit margin or a sales target, it is very hard to establish incentive pay programs for government workers. To have a pay-for-performance compensation scheme, one must be able to define and measure superior performance. In business, profits or sales are objective measures that can be used to set incentive pay. But one cannot do that in government, because these measures do not exist. Even trying to measure performance by the number of people served in government does not work, because people come in for government service at will as they need to, not because of anything a government worker has been doing. As a result, you cannot generally run government like a business by using compensation schemes to create performance incentives. It simply does not work that way.

Businesses also can use the tool of the cost-benefit analysis more effectively than governments. If I am running a business and I start a new product line and the expenses exceed the revenues, then I know that I might want to discontinue the product. But in government, the cost-benefit analysis is not always applicable for a variety of reasons. First, in government we do not always do things because they are cost effective. Government may try simply to help people, regardless of whether it is cost efficient. Second, with many government initiatives, it is often very hard to get reliable data on the benefits because they may be qualitative. Indeed, in many cases good data on cost effectiveness, whether mostly quantitative or qualitative, may not even exist, because the impact may run deep in the economy or society in a way that is simply not measurable, even if someone wanted to spend the money to measure it. It should be noted that there is a dark side to this aspect of things. Politicians can get away with enacting bad laws and programs because it is sometimes very hard to quantify afterwards what the impact is.

Business is different from government in another way. Business needs to be flexible and nimble so that it can respond quickly to changing market conditions. Government, on the other hand, is supposed to provide continuity and stability over a long period of time. As a result, governments tend to be very slow to change.

Business decision making is also very different from government decision making. In government, at least in the democratic United States, power is diffused among many different entities and people. We have a strong traditional belief that concentrating power in a few people is dangerous and can result in bad decision making. Businesses tend to be much more autocratic. In addition, in government there is often, though not always, a political element to be considered in the context of the decision making. Political decisions can be somewhat distorted because they do not seem to be based on the kind of right-versus-wrong standard that business decisions are judged by. I would argue that the best decision making in government is totally apolitical, and many decisions are made that way. Those who operate below the political level, the career bureaucrats, have less to gain from being political than those who operate at the political level.

Government differs from a business in a legal respect also. In business you can do anything you want to unless the law prohibits it. In government, you cannot do anything without legal authorization, although authority can both be express in the language of the statute and implied from that language. As a result, we should not expect government to be as innovative as business. It cannot be. Imagines a world in which government bureaucrats just made up things in their head and did them. In reality, we don't want government to innovate in the same way that businesses do.

Business differs from government in that it is easier to fire someone in the private sector than it is to fire someone in government. This makes it harder to manage people and to improve services over time. A related issue is that it is harder in government than in business to reorganize and reconfigure jobs to meet a changing environment.

Business also differs from government in that in business, there are usually a lot of competitors, while the government is usually acting as a monopoly. When you have competitors, you have to sharpen up your own execution to stay alive and keep current. Government monopolies do not have this outside pressure that requires them to continue to improve, and as a result they tend to stagnate.

Because government is so different from business, we should be skeptical of people who claim they want to run the government like a business. Of course, there are some similarities between government and business. To that extent, we can run them with the same best practices. You have the hiring and management of employees; you have budgeting; you have the need to try to improve productivity; you have a duty to serve customers well. But beyond the things that are common to almost all organizations, government is really nothing like a business.

Some businesspeople deeply resent the government. I think this is the wrong attitude. To be a successful businessman, you need to live in an environment that is conducive to a working market system. That means that the government must provide enforcement of property rights and contract rights. It means that the government must provide basic security and infrastructure. It means that the government must not be corrupt. There must be a level playing field for businesses to operate on, and the government must remain impartial and not pick winners and losers. Businesses need workers, and many of them must have at least some public school training. Fundamentally, businesspeople need at least part of what the government offers. Does that mean that all parts of our modern government help business? Of course not. The point is that we should not claim that government does nothing for a businessperson. My father was a real estate developer, and he always gave the credit for his success to being lucky enough to be an American citizen and to be part of the American system. He didn't claim to build the railroad all by himself.

We can run the government like a business to the extent possible, but in general we must run government like a government.

Chapter 21

Dealing with the Government

In dealing with a government agency, the first thing to consider is jurisdiction. Does the agency you are talking to have jurisdiction over the problem that you want to solve? If not, you're wasting your time. The other jurisdictional question is whether the agency you are talking about has the power to solve the problem that you want to solve. The government operates with limited powers. Fortunately, these questions are normally easily answered by the agency itself. If an agency says that it can't help you, then you should listen to it. Those in the executive branch have had people try to get them to overturn decisions by courts. But since the courts decide last, the executive branch has no power to overturn a court decision. Again, the agency can tell you whether you are barking up the right tree or not.

When writing a letter to the government, be brief. Those of us who work in the government often see long letters in which people try to tell their whole life story. You have to focus in on the facts that are relevant to your concern, and that will be something far less than your whole life story.

What should you do if you get into a dispute with the government? The first thing to realize is that the cards are stacked against you because the government has a lot of power and a certain amount of discretion. That said, government is all about the rule of law, so that there are, in fact, certain things that even the government cannot get away with doing. My experience with government people is that they are generally a decent bunch, but not all of them are that smart. So what you are hoping to do is to locate someone in the relevant government agency who seems like a relatively smart and reasonable person, and then make your case in a coherent letter. It doesn't do much good to rant and rave. In the end, the agency is going to make the decision it wants to make, and, absent manifest illegality, you're probably just going to have to live with it. If there is a formal appeals process by which you can challenge the agency decision, then follow the instructions carefully and do not try to short-circuit the process. One thing government workers do not like is when someone makes work for them, so try to be considerate and reasonable in terms of the amount of trouble that you create.

Sometimes people will try to elevate their dispute above the agency level by copying high-level politicians. Generally, these letters to politicians find their way back to the agency for input and advice to the politician by the agency. Politicians don't necessarily have the time to get inside all of the public complaints that arise, and so they tend to be deferential to the agency determination. I'm not saying that elevating a dispute will never work for you, but it should be undertaken only if there is something about your dispute that would be of particular interest to the politician that you are talking about. Once agencies make the decision, it is a good idea to stop fighting, because the chances that they are going to change their mind once they have already examined the issue is remote.

If you are trying to influence a matter of public policy, the way to approach a politician is to make him understand how supporting your position can win him votes or contributions, not just why it might be a good idea generally. Normally, if I am advocating on an issue of public policy, I take the time to see who else has advocated on the issue in the past and try to get them to buy into my viewpoint before going to politicians. The reason is that these kinds of advocates and stakeholders will be among those testifying on any related legislation when it happens, so it is a good idea to have them on board first. Since public policy requires support, you have think in advance whether there are going to be constituencies that support your policy that can beat the constituencies that will stand against it. Sometimes the deck is so stacked against you up front that it doesn't make sense to spend a lot of time pursuing the issue.

All of that said, as someone who has worked in the government, I can tell you that it is always useful to hear the perspective of the public on issues. The comments made by the public tend to stay in your memory when you are a government official. The question is whether you can really offer a government official information that he doesn't already know that can make a difference in how he does his job.

My approach in running a small business is not to call attention to myself. I want to remain invisible to the government to the extent possible so it doesn't bother me too much. So I just pay my taxes and generally keep quiet. I suggest that this is a good approach for most businesses. What do you as a citizen-advocate is another matter.

Chapter 22

Putting It All Together

People seek meaning in their lives. I would suggest that besides doing things for oneself, meaning can come from doing things for other people, whether they be your own family and friends, your business customers, or the public you serve as a government official. The idea is to serve a purpose that is larger than just yourself. I think that most people have a need for this kind of altruism, because it makes them feel good about themselves. Meaning can also come from religion, because religion creates a larger context to history by suggesting that all the things that we do in the course of history can serve a larger purpose, which is God's purpose.

A lifelong search for knowledge is also something that can help you make sense of things. There is an old Latin phrase that says that knowledge is power. If two people have unequal knowledge, then the person who has superior knowledge probably has power over the person with inferior knowledge. For this selfish reason, you should continue to seek knowledge at all times. But there is also a larger purpose to be served by becoming informed. We cannot be positively contributing citizens of a democracy unless we are well informed.

Another Latin phrase which is worth remembering translates to "Time devours all." Because we have limited time on Earth, our choices about what we do with that time matter, and it is those choices which define us.

Everyone has a choice whether to see himself as a victim of circumstances and other people or to see himself as the author of his own destiny. In general, people who take full personal responsibility for themselves and take control of their lives will do better than people that don't. If you add to the view of yourself as the "master of your own destiny" some persistence and commitment, then positive things can happen. In all things, emphasize action over passivity. You can read any number of self-help books, but the basic premise is always the same. They all say that your thoughts and attitudes can determine the outcomes in your life. That is why you have to monitor your own thinking and make sure it is the kind of thinking that will lead to success. If I meet a billionaire philanthropist who attributes his success to his belief in Mickey Mouse, then my first question is: how do I find out about this Mickey Mouse guy? In other words, if your belief system does positive things and gets you to behave in the way you want to behave, whether it is true or not is not the main point. Conversely, even if you have a belief that is true, if it creates negative consequences for you, then you should get rid of it.

www.ingramcontent.com/pod-product-compliance
Lightning Source LLC
Chambersburg PA
CBHW051325170526
45166CB00002B/692